MW01029037

A Concise Guide to Personality Disorders

A Concise Guide to Personality Disorders

Joel Paris

AMERICAN PSYCHOLOGICAL ASSOCIATION
WASHINGTON, DC

Published by
American Psychological Association
750 First Street, NE
Washington, DC 20002
www.apa.org

To order
APA Order Department
P.O. Box 92984
Washington, DC 20090-2984
Tel: (800) 374-2721; Direct: (202) 336-5510
Fax: (202) 336-5502; TDD/TTY: (202) 336-6123
Online: www.apa.org/pubs/books
E-mail: order@apa.org

In the U.K., Europe, Africa, and the Middle East, copies may be ordered from
American Psychological Association
3 Henrietta Street
Covent Garden, London
WC2E 8LU England

Typeset in Minion by Circle Graphics, Inc., Columbia, MD

Printer: Maple Press, York, PA
Cover Designer: Berg Design, Albany, NY

The opinions and statements published are the responsibility of the authors, and such opinions and statements do not necessarily represent the policies of the American Psychological Association.

Library of Congress Cataloging-in-Publication Data

Paris, Joel, 1940- , author.
  A concise guide to personality disorders / by Joel Paris.
    p. ; cm.
  Includes bibliographical references and index.
  ISBN 978-1-4338-1981-0 — ISBN 1-4338-1981-3
  I. American Psychological Association, issuing body. II. Title.
  [DNLM: 1. Personality Disorders. WM 190]
  RC473.P56
  616.85'81—dc23
                          2014043625

British Library Cataloguing-in-Publication Data
A CIP record is available from the British Library.

Printed in the United States of America
First Edition

http://dx.doi.org/10.1037/14642-000

This book is dedicated to the clinicians and researchers
with whom I have collaborated on understanding
and treating personality disorders.

Contents

Acknowledgments   ix

Introduction   3

Part One: General Issues

1. Why the Diagnosis of Personality Disorder Is Difficult   11

2. Traits, Disorders, and the *DSM–5*   23

3. Etiology   41

4. Prevalence, Precursors, and Outcome   55

Part Two: Specific Disorders

5. Antisocial Personality Disorder   65

6. Borderline Personality Disorder   73

7. Narcissistic Personality Disorder   91

8. Other Personality Disorders   99

Part Three: Treatment

9. Psychopharmacology   109

10. Psychotherapies   119

11. Management   137

12. Summary and Future Directions   153

CONTENTS

References   161

Index   187

About the Author   195

Acknowledgments

Michael Bond and Robert Biskin read an earlier version of this text and made many useful suggestions for improving it. I am also grateful to the peer reviewers and to Beth Hatch of the American Psychological Association, who recommended changes that have been included in the final version.

A Concise Guide to Personality Disorders

Introduction

Personality disorders (PDs) are commonly encountered in practice, but their management is challenging. Patients with these diagnoses can be described as the "stepchildren" of the mental health professions, the patients we have to take care of, even if we would rather not. However, one message of this book is that some forms of PD have a good prognosis and many (but not all) patients can be treated effectively. These conditions are no more mysterious or problematic than psychoses, mood disorders, or any other major group of mental illnesses. However, treating this population requires a wide range of knowledge and skill in biological, psychological, and social domains.

To provide effective therapy, you first have to recognize the problem. In many patients, PD goes undiagnosed. Clinical psychologists may prefer to diagnose anxiety and depression because they have tools designed to

http://dx.doi.org/10.1037/14642-001
A Concise Guide to Personality Disorders, by J. Paris

deal with those problems. One has to wonder whether psychiatrists tend to avoid making these diagnoses because they prefer to prescribe medication. Yet all mental health professionals need to understand the difference between transient symptoms and lifelong dysfunction.

This having been said, making a diagnosis of PD requires a certain level of skill. The construct is defined by the *Diagnostic and Statistical Manual of Mental Disorders* (5th edition; *DSM–5;* American Psychiatric Association, 2013) as an enduring, inflexible, and pervasive pattern of inner experience and behavior that begins in late adolescence or early adulthood and that continues to impede functioning in work and relationships over many years. However, clinicians have to make judgment calls, such as how enduring the personality pattern is and the extent to which it impedes functioning. As this book will show, there is no absolute boundary between variations in normal personality and PD. However, some PDs have striking symptoms that may be mistaken for other categories of mental illness.

WHY I WROTE THIS BOOK

The primary focus of my professional career has been patients with PDs. Some of my colleagues try to avoid these cases—in vain, because they are common in practice (unless, of course, you entirely ignore the role of personality in psychopathology). I also have colleagues who think these patients are just too difficult. I find the problems they present fascinating and challenging, but there is no easy fix, either through medication or psychotherapy.

When I began to treat patients with PD, I was not satisfied with what were then the most influential theories, explaining personality pathology as a result of an unhappy childhood. I saw many patients with traumatic childhoods who grew up to be normal. I also saw patients with severe PDs who had suffered little more than misunderstanding.

I was curious to find out more about PDs, so after almost 15 years of clinical practice and teaching, I started a second career as a researcher. This meant returning to my roots in psychology (my undergraduate major). I was fortunate to be able to collaborate with psychologists trained in research. I had the added benefit of having practiced psychiatry on some of the sickest patients that mental health professionals see.

I entered the PD field just as it began to take off. The International Society for the Study of Personality Disorders was founded in 1987 and held its first meeting in 1988 (a 25th anniversary conference was held in 2013). The first issue of the *Journal of Personality Disorders* was published in 1987, and there are now two other print journals that focus on PD (*Personality Disorders: Theory, Research, and Treatment* and *Personality and Mental Health*). Attending scientific meetings over the years, I have met stimulating colleagues from all over the world, from whom I have learned much. Researchers in the same area tend to be spread around but form a kind of "invisible college"—we often see more of each other than colleagues from the same university. There are not many of us, only about 200 active PD researchers worldwide. I am proud to be of these happy few.

As a clinician, a teacher, and a researcher, I am also pleased to say that interest in PDs is definitely on the rise. Research on PDs has become much more active in the past 30 years, moving the field from clinical speculation to solid empirical investigation; since 1987, more than 20,000 articles reporting empirical research have been published. However, clinicians in practice, as well as many academics, continue to be reluctant to recognize PDs or to offer patients the specific forms of treatment they need. In this book, I try to explain why and give reasons why minds need to be changed.

Despite a rapidly developing knowledge base, PD remains mysterious in many ways. The goal of this book is to review what we know, what we don't know, and what the current state of knowledge implies for treatment. I aim to bring clinicians up-to-date with the latest research on PD and to suggest management strategies that are consistent with that evidence base. I will show that even if we cannot always provide definitive treatment for these patients, we can reduce distress and promote functioning.

This book differs in three important ways from previous guides to the management of PDs. First, it provides an evidence-based perspective. It makes no sense to depend entirely on clinical impressions when thousands of research papers have been published. Where there is strong evidence, I review the literature and suggest how it can be integrated into practice.

Where there is little or no literature, I say less and suggest where further investigation is needed. Although it is not possible to write a book on this subject without relying on clinical experience, I make clear what is science and what is opinion.

Second, this book focuses on clinical problems that have been examined in systematic research. Because borderline PD (BPD) is by far the best-studied disorder (nearly 7,000 articles published since 1987), it is the main subject of this book. Antisocial PD also has a large literature (nearly 5,000 articles over the same period), but I still have more to say about BPD because, as we now know, it is usually treatable. BPD is a problem that challenges clinicians, but there is strong and growing research supporting effective therapy of these patients. When a larger body of data emerges on other PDs, we may develop treatment packages for them as well.

Third, this book argues that clinicians need to replace systems of therapy identified by acronyms and associated with charismatic founders. Even if some of these methods are evidence based, we need to adopt integrative, eclectic methods that combine the best ideas from all schools. A single paradigm, called *psychotherapy*, is needed to heal these divisions. An integrative approach is well supported by research and also makes the most practical sense.

THE STRUCTURE OF THIS BOOK

This book consists of three parts. The first is devoted to general issues about PDs. Chapter 1 addresses thorny problems of definition and the uncertain boundary between PD and personality. Chapter 2 focuses on the relationships between traits and disorders and assesses the advantages and disadvantages of proposals to revised or replace the *DSM* system. Chapter 3 examines etiology and risk factors, and Chapter 4 reviews prevalence and outcome.

The second part of the book is devoted to specific PD categories: Chapter 5 on antisocial PD, Chapter 6 on BPD, Chapter 7 on narcissistic PD, Chapter 8 on other PDs (schizotypal, schizoid, paranoid, histrionic, avoidant, obsessive–compulsive, dependent, and PD, not otherwise specified).

The third part of the book concerns treatment. Chapter 9 examines the efficacy of pharmacotherapy, and Chapter 10 reviews evidence concerning the various psychotherapies developed for PD. Chapter 11 presents a general approach to management, with emphasis on the borderline category. Finally, Chapter 12 summarizes what we know about PD and what we need to find out.

ONE

GENERAL ISSUES

Why the Diagnosis of Personality Disorder Is Difficult

This chapter provides an overview of problems in the diagnosis and classification of personality disorders (PDs). Its overall theme is that PDs are both underdiagnosed and underrecognized in clinical practice.

PDs CARRY STIGMA

The PD construct can meet with a surprising level of resistance, sometimes approaching hostility. At the 2011 Annual Convention of the American Psychiatric Association, a well-known psychoanalyst-researcher told an audience that diagnosing patients with borderline PD (BPD) is no more valid than calling them "jerks." In another session at the same meeting, a biological psychiatrist who prefers to see BPD as a form of "bipolarity" stated that a diagnosis of PD is an insult he would never dream of inflicting on a patient.

http://dx.doi.org/10.1037/14642-002
A Concise Guide to Personality Disorders, by J. Paris

Why does PD arouse so much opposition? Stigma is certainly part of the answer, but isn't there at least as much stigma associated with psychosis or depression? The answer is, not necessarily. Stigma is rooted in the fear of having a mental illness oneself. When I try to explain my work to other professionals, the predictable response is, "How do I know I don't have one of these diagnoses?" Most of us are sure we are not psychotic. We are not so sure we don't have a PD. Rejecting the construct protects us from that possibility.

Mental disorder has always carried stigma and probably always will (Corrigan, 2000). Losing an arm or a leg is sad, but it doesn't affect the integrity of the self. In contrast, losing one's mind is much more threatening. That is why being called "crazy" has always been an insult. The implication is that you are somehow *responsible* for losing your mind.

We all have a personality, but we may wonder, based on feedback from others, whether we have a bad one. The concept of PD is threatening because we are unable to protect ourselves from this specter. According to a concept called a *fundamental attribution bias* (Jones & Harris, 1967), we see other people's misbehavior as reflecting their personality, whereas our own mistakes only reflect difficult situations. This is why PD constructs can become insults. People who are selfish or have big egos may be called narcissistic, whereas perfectionists may be called obsessive–compulsive. Can any of us be sure we do not have a PD? Evidently not.

The other part of the reluctance to diagnose PD is the perception that these disorders are incurable. That is why clinicians prefer to focus on symptoms for which they have effective tools to treat. It is certainly true that PDs begin early in life and affect psychosocial functioning over many years. However, research shows that most patients get better with time (Gunderson et al., 2011). It also shows that patients with BPD, once thought incurable, are much more treatable than previously thought (Paris, 2010a).

I aim to reduce stigma when I explain PD to patients. I tell them that the diagnosis describes people who can't get their life together, either in relationships or at work. This capsule message usually gets across because it fits with what they already know about themselves. It also offers hope. I inform patients that they will probably improve with time but that treatment can make recovery go faster. Both statements are evidence based.

The problem is that many, if not most, patients with PDs are mis-diagnosed (Zimmerman, Dalrymple, Chelminski, Young, & Galione, 2010). They most often tend to be seen, at least initially, as having mood disorders. PD is only considered when treatment for depression or bipolarity fails.

An even more serious problem is that patients with PDs are being treated inappropriately (and unsuccessfully) with medications. This is not entirely the fault of physicians or of the psychologists who request medical consultation. Unfortunately, by the time patients meet mental health professionals, they may have been socialized to consider themselves as suffering from "chemical imbalances." For this reason, some patients may insist on retaining a mood disorder diagnosis and request a medication cocktail. Another current trend in practice is diagnosing PD patients with attention-deficit/hyperactivity disorder (ADHD), which also leads to a prescription. Those who have failed to respond to several medication trials may be more open to accepting a diagnosis of PD.

I encourage patients, if they have not already done so, to use the Internet to read about PD. Doing so can make them feel validated. Many are actually relieved to receive a diagnosis that corresponds to their life experience. They know intuitively that their personality doesn't work and that depression is the result, not the cause, of their troubles. Many have had the experience of being unsuccessfully treated for other diagnoses with inappropriate forms of treatment.

Successful treatment of PD would be more common if the educated public knew more about the subject, but explaining what *personality disorder* means to nonprofessionals is challenging. On one occasion, I was interviewed on the radio and offered narcissistic PD as an example. My host replied, "But I'm also a bit of a ham!" More recently, I was asked to explain my research to a group of basic scientists working at my hospital. Once again, the almost universal reaction was defensive and fearful: "How do I know that this doesn't describe me?" I have learned to concentrate on the self-harm and suicide attempts associated with BPD so that everyone knows the subject is mental illness, not ordinary life. Even so, stigma gets in the way of the message.

If the fear of losing control of one's own mind is the main cause of the stigma associated with mental disorders, then PDs have to be particularly threatening. When disorders are exaggerations of normal traits, we recognize ourselves, albeit in a distorting mirror.

Even when PD presents as an alien state, readily recognized as an illness, the construct does not always meet with acceptance. For example, emergency department doctors sometimes hate patients with BPD. I have heard them say, "I am already busy with so many people who are sick for no fault of their own, so why should I have to spend time treating patients whose illness is self-inflicted?" What these professionals are missing is that these patients experience intense suffering, which they express through impulsive actions.

WHY PD CANNOT BE EASILY EXPLAINED AT THE LEVEL OF NEUROSCIENCE

The neuroscience model that dominates the contemporary practice of psychiatry works against the recognition and treatment of PDs. Ironically, reliance on brain research was a strategy developed by the mental health professions to get around stigma. Psychiatry now views mental disorders as brain disorders, and its most influential paradigm redefines practice as the clinical application of neuroscience (Insel & Quirion, 2005). Yet this point of view leads to problems, most obviously to the tendency to prescribe drugs to all patients.

Clinical psychology has also been influenced by cognitive neuroscience, which has provided evidence that therapy works by changing brain function (Trull & Prinstein, 2012). Unfortunately, some clinical psychologists have adopted the same point of view as psychiatrists, sending more and more patients in therapy to physicians for consultation—with the almost guaranteed result that medication will be prescribed.

Although it is true that mental illness is a product of the brain, it does not follow that disorders can readily be explained on a neural level. As later chapters in this book show, there are biological risk factors for PDs, but their effects depend on their interaction with the environment. Biological *reductionism* fails to acknowledge the importance of psychosocial factors in development. A widely quoted article by Insel and Quirion (2005) suggested that psychiatry abolish itself by becoming a part of neurology, but the words *psychology* or *psychotherapy* cannot be found in the text. So much for the biopsychosocial model!

Reductionistic theories, in which mental disorders are seen as "nothing but" brain disorders, remove agency from patients. In a fully deterministic model, psychotherapy would be next to impossible. Patients may not be considered responsible for getting better but are viewed as victims of chemical imbalances and aberrant neurocircuitry. To recover, patients would only be asked to be passive recipients of pharmacological treatment.

This model is reasonably appropriate for the psychoses, in which theory and practice would benefit from more, not less, data based on neurobiology. It is wrong, however, for other mental disorders, such as mild to moderate depression, substance abuse, and PDs. In each of these conditions, patients are not the victims of chemistry but of choices. People who fail at work and relationships have cognitive misconceptions, difficult emotions, and problematic behaviors that cannot be reduced to the activity of neurotransmitters. It is also wrong from a philosophical point of view. Therapists cannot work effectively with patients without believing in the existence of free will.

Our current knowledge base about psychopathology is, unfortunately, insufficient to explain mental illness (Uher & Rutter, 2012). That conclusion certainly applies to PD, which remains in so many ways a mystery. However, we do know enough to say that PDs, although partly shaped by biological factors, are strongly influenced by psychological and social risks. The attempt to take stigma away from PD by making it an epiphenomenon of neurobiology oversimplifies an enormously complex problem.

PDs ARE OFTEN MISDIAGNOSED

Despite its clinical importance, the diagnosis of PD is often missed. If practitioners are not well trained to manage these patients, they may prefer to call them something else. Another reason for missing PD is that clinicians tend to have a preference for diagnoses that are currently "hot."

Let us consider some examples. First, because most patients who see therapists are notably unhappy, it is tempting to diagnose them with depression. The *Diagnostic and Statistical Manual of Mental Disorders*

(5th edition; *DSM–5;* American Psychiatric Association, 2013) criteria set the bar much too low for a diagnosis of major depression (five of nine symptoms for only 2 weeks), greatly encouraging overdiagnosis (Paris, 2013a). Focusing on episodes of low mood in patients with PD ignores more important long-term behavioral patterns. By definition, these patients have had problems for most of their lives.

Second, the faddishly popular diagnosis of bipolar disorder has been used to account for many of the phenomena associated with PD, most particularly moodiness (Paris, 2012). If you follow the guidelines in *DSM–5,* bipolarity requires clear periods of mania or hypomania, but clinicians may invoke this diagnosis in all patients who only have a mood instability that indicates emotion dysregulation.

Third, the diagnosis of posttraumatic stress disorder (PTSD) has been applied to patients who have been exposed to significant trauma. Yet this preference fails to take into account that PTSD has a characteristic symptom profile and that most people who have experienced trauma do not develop the disorder (McNally, 2003). Applying this label to every patient who has experienced significant adversity strays from diagnostic precision and is misleading.

Fourth, ADHD, another diagnosis that has become a fad, is currently being used to explain a wide variety of clinical problems (Batstra & Frances, 2012). Even though many other conditions, such as anxiety and depression, affect attention, it is tempting to make a diagnosis believed to respond predictably to stimulant medication.

Specialists in any group of mental disorders tend to be enthusiastic about their ideas. They may see the conditions they study everywhere and diagnose them all too freely. This is the case for all the currently popular diagnoses just mentioned. As a PD specialist, I try to bend over backward to avoid overdiagnosis, particularly when problems are situational rather than lifelong. If everyone who has serious trouble with work or relationships is seen as having a PD, at least half of us could meet criteria, making the concept so broad that it would lose meaning.

The misdiagnosis of PD feeds into the reluctance to make these diagnoses, even when they are obvious. PDs may be complex, but they can describe clinical pictures parsimoniously. Why give patients multiple symptomatic diagnoses when a single PD category covers most of the same ground? Moreover, some PDs, most particularly BPD, describe patients who are treatable. Making the diagnosis provides information that can be used to guide treatment planning.

PDs ARE COMPLEX

One of the main sources of resistance to diagnosing PD is the complexity of the construct. Mood is simple, but personality is complicated. By and large, simplicity trumps complexity and leads to ideas that are clinically seductive.

The ideology of neuroscience is a good example. It favors disordered chemistry or neuroconnectivity (or a combination of these) as explanations for mental illness. Although these mechanisms are not really simple, they simplify the problem by being reductionistic. Considering interactions between brain mechanisms and environmental factors introduces a much greater level of complexity. We now know that neurobiology is not just a given and that experience changes the brain (Rutter, 2006).

Even at a neural level, the task of accounting for behavior is, to say the least, formidable. The brain is unbelievably complex, with 100 billion neurons and trillions of synapses. This makes the utility of reducing mental disorder to cellular mechanisms doubtful. It makes more sense to study the mind at its own level while keeping neural mechanisms well in mind.

PD can only be understood at multiple levels of analysis by examining complex interactions between temperament and life experiences. The attempt to turn complexity into simplicity leads to serious clinical problems. A biomedical approach, offering drugs for every symptom, ignores the cognitive, emotional, and behavioral patterns that make patients unhappy. Psychologists who focus only on symptoms also do so at the expense of understanding life histories. Thus, even if patients with PDs are sad, moody, or fearful—as they often are, given their troubled lives—they cannot be treated with standard methods developed for common mental disorders.

One often hears that PDs may remit when mood disorders are treated, so one should "defer" making these diagnoses when patients are depressed.

Actually, several lines of evidence refute that conclusion. One is that patients who also have a PD do not respond well to standard treatment for depression (Newton-Howes, Tyrer, & Johnson, 2006). Another is that patients with PDs almost always continue to meet criteria even when depression remits (Lopez-Castroman et al., 2012). These findings contradict the idea that PDs are nothing but atypical mood disorders, as some researchers have proposed (Akiskal, 2004). If only it were true that antidepressants and mood stabilizers could put PDs into remission! As a recent Cochrane report showed, research consistently indicates that they cannot (Stoffers et al., 2010). It is therefore better to use a complex construct like PD that does justice to clinical problems than to replace it with a simpler one, like mood disorder, that does not.

To differentiate PD from mood disorder, one needs to take a careful history of life events over many years. Patients with mood disorders have episodes of illness that derail their functioning for defined periods of time. In contrast, patients with PDs have had serious problems continuously for years, usually beginning in adolescence (or earlier). Patients with mood disorders suffer from depressive (or hypomanic) episodes that temporarily interfere with their lives but leave the self intact. Patients with PDs have pathology that lies in the self and may never have been "normal" enough to get "back to normal."

SEPARATING MILD PDs FROM NORMAL VARIATIONS IN PERSONALITY

For PD to be considered a legitimate diagnosis, it must be as well defined as any other mental disorder and distinguished from normal variations in personality. Strange to say, the *DSM* did not include a formal overall definition of PD until its fourth edition (American Psychiatric Association, 1994). That definition, retained in *DSM–5*, emphasizes that PD is chronic, beginning in late adolescence or early adulthood, and impedes functioning in work and relationships over many years. Unfortunately, language such as *enduring*, *inflexible*, and *pervasive* gives the impression of incurability. As this book shows, that is far from the case.

One of the problems with the *DSM* system is the way it defines PDs as categories. There are 10 of them in the *DSM–5*, of which only two or three (borderline, antisocial, and schizotypal) have solid research behind them. Moreover, anyone who has a PD that does not fit any of the 10 has to be diagnosed as personality disorder, not otherwise specified (now called in *DSM–5*, PD, Unspecified). This is the most common diagnosis in practice (Coccaro, Nayyer, & McCloskey, 2012), because only about half of all patients who meet overall PD criteria meet specific criteria for the currently listed categories (Zimmerman, Rothschild, & Chelminski, 2005). Of those who do meet criteria, patients in clinical settings often meet criteria for more than one (Nurnberg et al., 1991). This shows that the current categorical system is not valid. Although every clinician can recognize diagnoses when they are typical and paradigmatic, many if not most patients fall between the cracks of the system. Moreover, given the polythetic nature of the system (i.e., requiring only a limited number of symptoms from a longer list), people with the same diagnosis can be quite different from each other.

One solution to this problem is to view PDs as *dimensional*, that is, as pathological amplifications of traits with a continuous relationship to normality. Trait psychology sees PDs in this way, rooted in the domains identified by research on normal personality. Using these models, one can quantify personality dimensions so that diagnosis depends on a cutoff that defines a point at which trait amplification reaches a pathological level. The most widely used schema is the five-factor model (FFM; Widiger & Costa, 2013), which has been the subject of an enormous amount of research. If PD represents an exaggerated set of personality traits that lead to dysfunction, then the FFM can be adapted for clinical use to describe patients with more precision than categorical diagnoses.

Why have clinicians been somewhat hesitant about adopting dimensional assessment as a diagnostic tool? The first reason is that practitioners are used to the algorithm-based categories of the *DSM*. Some of these categories have a strong research base, and diagnosis can be a distinct help in guiding treatment. A second is that even though quantitative data provide more information, clinical decisions are categorical. A third is that given the time restrictions of practice, it may not always be practical to give patients questionnaires, even in computerized forms.

The dimensional approach has a large body of research in normal populations, but it may or may not be a useful guide to treatment in clinical settings. Almost all research thus far on the treatment of PDs has concerned patients with categorically diagnosable disorders (e.g., BPD), although it is possible that specific psychotherapies based on dimensions could eventually be developed. Categorical diagnoses of PD do not tell us how to conduct therapy but often point to the likelihood of failure to respond to certain types of interventions, in both pharmacological treatment and psychotherapy (Newton-Howes et al., 2006).

The larger problem is that all mental disorders require a cutoff between normality and pathology. Sometimes the difference is obvious, as when patients are psychotic or suffer from a profound depression, but in less severe disorders, the cutoff for diagnosis may not be so clear. In such cases, the question arises as to whether one is looking at a mental illness or a normal psychological reaction.

Wakefield (1992) proposed a way to cut this Gordian knot. His idea was that patients with mental disorders must be characterized by *harmful dysfunction.* In other words, problems have to involve distress or impairment, as well as the failure of a psychological mechanism to perform its naturally designed function. Determining harm and dysfunction still requires judgment calls, however, based more on clinical experience than on empirical data demonstrating construct validity.

This is also a problem in the clinical applicability of trait dimensional models. Almost anyone might be diagnosed with a PD if he or she has significant dysfunction in a major area of life. (Most of us have at least some degree of dysfunction in work or relationships.) The more broad the definition, the more likely it is that people with normal variation will be labeled as disordered. A definition of disorder that is too broad would also not be a useful guide to treatment.

A more precise definition of PD would be needed to describe homogeneous groups of patients. For example, the decision as to whether traits interfere with function in a clinically significant way could be arbitrary.

Keeping cutoff points conservative helps to prevent diagnostic inflation. A narrower definition of PD would also be important for research. If criteria are applied scrupulously, then patient groups become more homogeneous, or at least have a heterogeneity that can be described systematically. Yet when patients suffer from only mild to moderate dysfunction, establishing a diagnosis is much more difficult. I return to this problem in Chapter 3, which critically examines research on the prevalence of PD. In summary, separating PD from normal variations in personality is problematic. When dysfunction is severe, the diagnosis will be clear. It is not so clear when dysfunction is mild to moderate. These problems are examined in more detail in the next chapter.

2

Traits, Disorders, and the *DSM–5*

This chapter examines where the boundaries lie between personality traits and disorders, whether categorical or dimensional systems are more valid, and whether the proposals that were made for the *Diagnostic and Statistical Manual of Mental Disorders* (5th ed.; *DSM–5;* American Psychiatric Association, 2013) would have had clinical benefit.

BOUNDARIES BETWEEN TRAITS AND DISORDERS

Everyone has a personality. *Trait* profiles describe behaviors, emotions, and cognitions that are unique to individuals. There is a good evolutionary reason why these characteristics should vary from one person to another. Like physical variations, traits are designed by natural selection to make survival more likely. However, the environment varies so much that traits that are adaptive in one setting will be maladaptive in others. Variation in nature is a hedge that makes survival possible in a range of environments.

http://dx.doi.org/10.1037/14642-003
A Concise Guide to Personality Disorders, by J. Paris

Thus, each of us has a unique personality profile, which is functional under some conditions but not others (Beck & Freeman, 2002). In other species (Réale, Reader, Sol, McDougall, & Dingemanse, 2007), aggressiveness and risk taking, or timidity and behavioral inhibition, can either be adaptive or maladaptive, depending on circumstances. The same principle applies to human beings. People who develop antisocial personality disorder (ASPD) in a deprived urban environment may have traits that could, in another context, make them into good soldiers. People whose shyness prevents them from finding a mate in modern society might do perfectly well in cultures where marriage is arranged.

Personality traits are usually measured using self-report questionnaires that have been validated in large community samples. There are several currently in use, but the largest body of research by far is on the five-factor model (FFM), which has also been adapted in a briefer version for clinical use (Widiger & Costa, 2013). The Big Five factors are *Neuroticism*, *Extraversion*, *Agreeableness*, *Conscientiousness*, and *Openness to Experience*, each of which can be divided into more specific facets. The Big Five have been shown to be valid in both community and clinical populations, in all social classes, and across cultures.

The main limitation of instruments that measure traits is their reliance on self-report. One cannot simply assume that people can describe themselves accurately, and some researchers have used informants to confirm these reports (Widiger & Costa, 2013). Kagan (2012) suggested that personality traits would best be described by using a convergence of multiple measures—questionnaires, ratings by other people, direct observation, and biological markers. Because multiple procedures are expensive, however, almost no one carries out research in that way.

Trait psychology also assumes there is no clear boundary to determine when traits end and disorder begins. In this view, personality disorder (PD) reflects an extreme and dysfunctional trait profile (Livesley, 2003). Thus, PD would be an analogue to medical phenomena such as the relation of blood sugar to diabetes or of blood pressure to hypertension. In these cases, one can mark a threshold for disorder on the basis of an increased likelihood of dysfunctional complications. However, there is no way to establish a definite cutoff between traits and disorders with external validity.

Another problem is that, as discussed in the previous chapter, if a dimensional approach defines PD so broadly, it might be hard to see who wouldn't have one. This would undermine the goal of getting clinicians to recognize these disorders. This is the same problem I ran into trying to explain PD to nonpsychiatric colleagues (maybe they had a point!). It is analogous to the question of the difference between sadness and depression (A. V. Horwitz & Wakefield, 2007) or between fear and anxiety (A. V. Horwitz & Wakefield, 2012). If we accept the broad definition of major depression used in the *DSM* system, in which 2 weeks of distress would be sufficient for a diagnosis that would affect half of the general population over a lifetime (Moffitt et al., 2010). This shows just how difficult it is to separate psychopathology from normality. Differences in degree eventually become differences in kind, and clinicians need categories to guide their treatment choices.

EGOSYNTONIC AND EGODYSTONIC ASPECTS OF PD

Much ink has been spilled, and much emotion expressed, as to whether PDs should be classified in terms of categories or dimensions. Those favoring categories see the dimensional alternative as obscure and lacking in clinical relevance. Those favoring dimensions see categories as arbitrary and unscientific. My own view is intermediate: Both systems have value, but we do not know enough to choose between them. At this point, although traits provide more information, some categories (borderline and antisocial) capture clinical syndromes that need to be identified.

Some of the confusion about the best way to classify PDs derives from the fact that there are two distinct aspects of PD. This distinction is based on the well-known description of mental disorders as either *egodystonic*, in which patients have symptoms they find troubling and alien, or as *egosyntonic*, in which patients consider their traits or symptoms to be normal (Hirschfeld, 1993). For example, obsessive–compulsive disorder (as opposed to obsessive–compulsive PD [OCPD]) is characterized by highly egodystonic thoughts, whereas patients with anorexia nervosa have an egosyntonic belief that their obsession with thinness is perfectly normal.

Applying this model to PDs, the more egosyntonic a disorder, the more readily it is classified dimensionally; the more egodystonic a disorder is, the more one should frame its psychopathology as a category. Thus, some disorders are almost entirely based on traits that are exaggerated but egosyntonic. The best examples are narcissistic PD (NPD) and OCPD. These categories describe people with amplified traits that get them into trouble in life but who do not usually recognize the nature of the problem. Patients with these diagnoses are insufficiently self-critical, often wondering why other people are not more like them. As described later in this book, in both disorders, there is a smooth and imperceptible transition between trait domains and diagnosable psychopathology.

In contrast, other PDs have predominant egodystonic features that are not fully explained by a trait profile. These symptoms, although associated with pathological traits, can describe a clinically important difference between trait domains and diagnosable disorders. The best example is borderline PD (BPD), in which patients are high in negative affectivity and impulsivity (Siever & Davis, 1991) and suffer from a wide variety of symptoms. Another example is avoidant PD, in which social anxiety produces a painful loneliness that leads patients to seek treatment (Sanislow, da Cruz, Gianoli, & Reagan, 2012).

There is some evidence that PDs with egodystonic features are, at least partially, discontinuous from their underlying trait profiles. In principle, the symptoms of any mental disorder can be scored dimensionally by considering them as traits (Krueger & Tackett, 2006). These models of psychopathology, in contrast to categorical systems, suggest a smooth progression from normality to pathology, and the absence of points of rarity among traits, subclinical phenomena, and diagnosable disorders (Kendell, 2002). Yet dimensional scores, such as the measurement of blood pressure in medicine, are still subject to categorical cutoffs. This is because clinical decision making in mental health practice remains a dichotomous procedure in that treatment decisions are usually based on the presence or absence of a defined condition. Moreover, severe mental disorders are generally heritable (Kendler & Prescott, 2006), have a more severe outcome than subclinical syndromes (Bedhiran & Sartorius, 1995), and often have a more specific response to treatment.

Because traits have stronger correlations than categories with neuro-biological measures (Insel et al., 2010), patients with PDs were considered as "poster children" for a dimensional approach in the proposals for *DSM–5*. However, there are no known consistent biomarkers for personality traits.

Moreover, studies of trait dimensions show that they sometimes capture only a portion of the variance in PD. Using data from the Longitudinal Study of Personality Disorders (a large sample of college students followed prospectively), Wright, Pincus, and Lenzenweger (2012) conducted regressions of traits on PD symptoms The results showed that considering symptoms as normally distributed resulted in a violation of model assumptions (too many subjects scored zero) and that results differed according to whether one was predicting the presence of PD or its severity.

Similarly, in a study in which PD diagnosis was scored by clinical ratings of *DSM* criteria (Zimmerman, Chelminski, Young, Dalrymple, & Martinez, 2013), dimensional scoring, based on counts of *DSM* criteria, added information in subclinical cases but not in cases without a diagnosis. This finding contradicts the assumption of a smooth progression from trait profiles to clinical pathology and suggests discontinuities between traits and PDs.

Also, the FFM may not be sufficiently sensitive to symptoms that are relatively uncommon in community samples, even when they are clinically important (Clark, 2007). Two studies using this system (Bagby, Costa, Widiger, Ryder, & Marshall, 2005; Morey et al., 2007) found that trait domains only partially accounted for the clinical features of PDs, particularly in disorders such as BPD, which are marked by egodystonic symptoms. Morey and Zanarini (2000), who also studied patients with BPD, reported that although the FFM's neuroticism scale accounted for some of the variance, it did not account for the most symptomatic aspects of the disorder (e.g., a wide range of impulsive behaviors).

All PDs share a common profile at the level of FFM trait domains, with high Neuroticism, low Conscientiousness, and low Agreeableness (Morey et al., 2007; Saulsman & Page, 2004). A more complex analysis of trait facets could be needed to account for clinical symptoms associated with PDs (Widiger & Mullins-Sweatt, 2009). We do not know if this approach is feasible or has clinical utility.

To resolve this problem, self-report instruments have been specifically designed to measure the trait dimensions that underlie PD. The Schedule for Nonadaptive and Adaptive Personality (Simms & Clark, 2006) and the Diagnostic Assessment of Personality Pathology (DAPP; Livesley, Jang, & Vernon, 1998) overlap with the FFM in most respects, and the DAPP has been factor analyzed into four domains that closely resemble the FFM. Both instruments differ from the FFM in that they make a point of assessing egodystonic symptoms such as self-harm. That behavioral pattern can be found in community populations (Kessler, Berglund, Borges, Nock, & Wang, 2005) but is more intermittent and not associated with the development of PD (Klonsky, 2007).

Measures of traits based entirely on self-report may not be ideal to assess features of PDs that are not seen as problematic by patients. For example, Cooper, Balsis, and Oltmanns (2012) found that a diagnosis of NPD was more accurate if informants were interviewed about patterns that patients themselves failed to recognize. Sometimes, observations scored by trained observers can pick up aspects of psychopathology that questionnaires miss, as Perry (1992) found when comparing of self-report instruments with semistructured interviews for diagnosis of PDs.

Other research supports the overall conclusion that PDs are an amalgam of traits and symptoms (Skodol et al., 2005). Long-term follow-up of patients with several PDs over 10 years (Gunderson et al., 2011) and of patients with BPD over 14 years (Zanarini, Frankenburg, Reich, & Fitzmaurice, 2012) has shown that these disorders have a unique trajectory over time in that traits remain stable, whereas symptoms tend to remit.

Egosyntonic and egodystonic features are overlapping but conceptually distinct domains of PD that are different in different categories of disorder. For example, BPD is a complex form of psychopathology that reflects multiple endophenotypes (Paris, 2007a) and that straddles externalizing and internalizing spectra of mental disorders (Røysamb et al., 2011). Thus, although BPD is rooted in trait profiles, it cannot be entirely reduced to them. The affective instability and impulsivity associated with this disorder does not explain why patients end up overdosing or wrist cutting. The construct of BPD goes beyond the quirks that differentiate one person from another. It describes problems that interfere with getting a life and keeping one.

Similarly, patients with avoidant personality have striking egodystonic features. Given their sensitivity, these patients feel they are right to fear social rejection. Even so, they may ask for help to overcome loneliness and isolation (Sanislow, da Cruz, Gianoli, & Reagan, 2012).

In contrast, let us consider two examples of PD categories that reflect extreme levels of traits, with few egodystonic symptoms. These categories can be understood as amplified and dysfunctional trait profiles, just as a dimensional model would predict.

The best example is NPD. Research suggests that high levels of trait narcissism are essentially equivalent to a diagnosis of NPD (Paris, 2013b; Pincus & Lukowitsky, 2010). The disorder is characterized by a grandiose view of the self, and patients meeting these criteria tend to maintain their self-image by blaming others for their problems. This makes the disorder highly egosyntonic, although patients can eventually be unhappy enough to seek treatment (Ronningstam, 2010).

A second example is OCPD. This construct is characterized by high levels of conscientiousness and perfectionism, and the disorder is essentially equivalent to high levels of compulsive traits (de Rues & Emmelkamp, 2012). OCPD patients may consider their own personality normal, regarding others as careless or sloppy (Samuel & Widiger, 2011). Thus the disorder tends to be egosyntonic, but because perfection is impossible, compulsive traits can create interpersonal difficulties.

Similar principles can be applied to other PDs with prominent egosyntonicity. Patients with paranoid PD believe they are perfectly right to be suspicious, and patients with schizoid PD are comfortable with being socially isolated. Patients with dependent PD believe they have a right to ask other people to take care of them. All these categories are exaggerated and dysfunctional traits that can readily be dimensionalized (Widiger & Costa, 2013).

ASPD is difficult to place in this model: It has mainly egosyntonic features, yet some of its egodystonic features resemble BPD (Gunderson, 2013; Paris, Chenard-Poirier, & Biskin, 2013). Thus, comorbid anxiety and mood disorders are associated with a significant risk (approximately 5%) for completed suicide (Ullrich & Coid, 2009). Patients with ASPD are well known for not seeking help and for justifying the most problematic behaviors. In its most severe form, psychopathy (Hare, 1999), there is little suffering. Even so, ASPD is a complex disorder, describing amplified trait dimensions (low conscientiousness, low agreeableness) as well as features (chronic criminality) that are qualitatively different from behaviors in normal population (Black, 2013a).

DSM–5: THE STORY OF A CONTROVERSY

The classification of PDs has long been problematic. Most patients don't fit existing categories, but dimensional scores don't always do justice to severe psychopathology.

Years before the *DSM–5* process was launched, the battle lines were already drawn. In 2004, I attended a 2-day conference in Washington, DC, at which the American Psychiatric Association asked a group of researchers to come up with a dimensional model for PD. Nobody could agree on how to do this. Some were proponents of the FFM, others favored dimensional models that included more measures of psychopathology, and others felt that the most well-researched categories should be retained. My view was that we didn't yet know enough to replace a familiar model, however flawed, with a new system that would have uncertain validity and clinical utility.

In the absence of any consensus, the next 9 years were marked by controversy, leading to an epic struggle. The *DSM–5* Task Force, led by a mood disorder researcher (David Kupfer from Pittsburgh) and an epidemiologist (Darryl Regier from the American Psychiatric Association), wanted a dimensional system of diagnosis because they believed that quantitative scores are closer to neurobiology. Trait psychologists had been arguing for such a system for decades.

The *DSM–5* Personality Disorders Work Group was therefore encouraged to come up with a dimensional model, but it could not ignore the large number of researchers who favored categories and who had based their careers on studying categories. The group also made some political errors. One was that it excluded the people who had worked on the fourth edition of the *DSM* (*DSM–IV;* American Psychiatric Association, 1994), most of whom weren't even consulted. (When *DSM–IV* was being prepared, I wasn't on the committee but, along with many others, was sent a copy of the draft and invited to make comments. Although I am sure this process had no impact on the outcome, it made me feel included.)

Total exclusion forced those who were not on committees to state their objections in journals. The most important example was a paper in *The American Journal of Psychiatry* (Shedler et al., 2010), which made it clear that all these experts considered a dimensional system a potential disaster. The fact that so many of the leading researchers on PD were against the work group's proposals was a major factor in its ultimate rejection.

Who, then, was included in the *DSM–5* process? Membership on the work group was wide ranging, including neuroscientists, clinical psychiatrists, and trait psychologists. I have great respect for the members of this group, although not all had extensive clinical experience. Another twist in the story is that some members, including the chair, Andrew Skodol, had been involved with the Collaborative Longitudinal Study of Personality Disorders, a multimillion-dollar project funded by the National Institute of Mental Health (Skodol et al., 2005). This was the largest study ever conducted on PD, and it examined long-term outcomes for four categories (BPD, schizotypal PD, avoidant PD, and OCPD). It may not have been an accident that none of these were ever slated for removal.

To the credit of the *DSM–5* Task Force, all proposals for change in the manual were posted on the Internet in February 2010. This procedure allowed nonmembers to comment, either in print or among themselves, on these ideas. Along with a number of others, I cosigned a letter to the PD work group outlining the problems with the proposal. However, this kind of feedback was totally ineffective. Committees have a life of their own, and their move to consensus has sometimes been called "groupthink." Members whom I had previously known to be agnostic about simple solutions to the problems of PD classification became almost religiously attached to the proposals developed by the work group and were bitterly disappointed when they failed.

THE *DSM–5* HYBRID PROPOSAL

A great deal of work went into creating a new classification of PDs for *DSM–5* that would be based on a clinical assessment of personality traits. It was proposed that diagnosis should be rooted in two basic features that can be scored dimensionally: significant impairments in self (identity or self-direction) and interpersonal (empathy or intimacy) functioning, as well as one or more pathological personality trait domains or trait facets. As in *DSM–IV*, impairments in personality functioning and the individual's personality trait profile would have to be relatively stable across time and consistent across situations. There was a problem, however: Although most of the research on trait dimensions has used self-report, *DSM–5* proposed that *clinicians* would be the ones to rate both traits and functioning, using a set of standard scales. Yet such ratings might not be reliable. The proposal was also a hybrid in that it allowed for dimensional diagnosis but allowed clinicians to infer categorical diagnoses from trait profiles.

The work group had not wanted to take sides in the long-running categorical–dimensional dispute, so a hybrid system attempted to combine both approaches, building categories on ratings of trait dimensions. Most of the procedures were dimensional—scores for PD characteristics as a whole, scores for functional levels, and ratings of trait profiles to define specific disorders. Six of the 10 categories listed in *DSM–IV* were retained, with two (schizoid and paranoid) folded into schizotypal PD and another two (histrionic and dependent) dropped entirely. Those that remained would be defined on the basis of trait domains to be rated by clinicians (Skodol et al., 2011), rather than on *DSM*-style algorithms (a list of characteristic features to be scored categorically).

Thus, the hybrid proposal attempted to satisfy both trait psychologists and the BPD researchers who wrote the article that appeared in *The American Journal of Psychiatry* (Shedler et al., 2010). In the end, as is the case for many compromises, the proposal satisfied no one. The word also went around that the work group was dysfunctional. John Livesley, a strong proponent of dimensional classification, resigned and published an article explaining why the hybrid system was incoherent and unscientific (Livesley, 2010).

The categorical–dimensional dispute was not the only problem for the work group's proposal. The *DSM–5* field trials, by design, avoided making direct comparisons between *DSM–IV* and *DSM–5*. Thus, there was no clear evidence of superiority for the new system. Furthermore, the only field trial that examined the reliability of diagnoses in *DSM–5* came up with equivocal results (Regier et al., 2013). Results at two sites showed that BPD was reliable in Toronto but not in Houston, a finding that was hardly reassuring.

Opinion was sharply divided on the merits of the hybrid system. Some felt that categories were getting short shrift (Gunderson, 2013). For others, like John Livesley, the system was not dimensional enough and should have dispensed with categories entirely. For still others, particularly members of the work group, it was the ideal solution to a complex problem, and its failure was a tragedy. For myself, the hybrid system was overly complex, lacking in both clinical utility and empirical support. The jury is still out on this proposal, which is now in Section III of *DSM–5* as an "alternative model" considered to require further research.

Because many experts supported the alternative model, let us examine it in a little more detail. It has a series of stages and procedures (American Psychiatric Association, 2013): (a) determining whether impairment in self (identity or self-direction) and interpersonal (empathy or intimacy) functioning is present; (b) rating the level of impairment on a Levels of Personality Functioning Scale; (c) determining whether one of the six defined types is present and recording the type and the severity of impairment; (d) if none of these are applicable, to record PD traits—specified (PDTS), list the trait domains that are applicable, and record the severity of impairment; and (e) if a more detailed personality profile is desired, evaluate the trait facets. At each of these steps, clinicians would be asked to use a Likert scale (1–5) for scoring. Thus, they could diagnose a PD, rate its severity, and then score levels of personality functioning.

All patients with PD would be rated on five personality trait domains: negative affectivity, detachment, antagonism, disinhibition versus compulsivity, and psychoticism. The first four resemble four of those described in the FFM, as well as by other personality schema. (The fifth factor in the

FFM, Openness to Experience, was omitted because it has little significance for psychopathology.) The fifth domain in *DSM–5*, psychoticism, does not appear in most trait models because it describes problems that are less common in community populations, but it is needed to describe patients with PD.

This was an ambitious undertaking that would probably require more time than most practitioners currently devote to diagnostic assessment. Moreover, each of these ratings required judgment calls to determine what is normal, what is extreme, and what is truly dysfunctional. There was also some unfamiliar terminology (e.g., integrity of self-concept, identity integration, self-directedness, complex and integrated representations of others). I have to wonder whether busy clinicians, who have been ignoring the precise instructions of the *DSM* system for the past three decades, could carry out such a demanding procedure.

My own opinion was that although many of the PD categories listed in *DSM–IV* suffer from serious problems in validity, the hybrid system could have made a bad situation even worse. I had several concerns. First, the system requires multiple ratings that even experts would have difficulty carrying out in a reliable way. Second, it uses obscure terminology (after 40 years in psychiatry, I am still hard put to say what the term *self* means). Third, overly complex concepts that appeal more to researchers might have made it harder to convince skeptical clinicians that patients suffer from PDs. The more difficult it is to make a diagnosis, the more likely it is that PDs will be ignored. Finally, because the hybrid system is only beginning to be examined in systematic research, it would be premature to adopt it unless it had the kind of empirical support that underpins the FFM.

The most serious problem for the hybrid system concerns clinical utility (Paris, 2013a). Although the proposal has received good ratings by selected groups of clinicians (Morey, Krueger, & Skodol, 2013), reliable multiple scoring on multiple dimensions would probably require intensive training. We already know that practitioners do not follow *DSM* in any systematic way. Practitioners neither remember nor consistently apply criteria listed in the *DSM* manual but make diagnoses that correspond to prototypes in their mind rather than to formal algorithms (Zimmerman & Mattia, 1999).

Another serious problem, one that has escaped many observers, is that clinician ratings of psychosocial dysfunction are particularly likely to be unreliable. These ratings would have been necessary to distinguish personality and PD. When you use self-report data that has been subject to psychometric investigation for decades or use structured interviews with established reliability, you can empirically determine cutoff points. Clinicians cannot be expected to get these issues right, however, and may either underestimate or overestimate the likelihood of a PD. Basing a diagnostic classification on clinical impressions could have been problematic.

Had the scientific case for the new system been stronger, it would have motivated all of us to do diagnosis differently, as happened when the third edition of the *DSM* (*DSM–III*; American Psychiatric Association, 1980) was published in 1980. Clinicians could be willing to learn complicated procedures, but they first have to be convinced that the evidence supporting them is unimpeachable. I have taught the *DSM–III* and *DSM–IV* for several decades and can attest to a lack of success in getting trainees to make reliable clinical ratings using either algorithms or quantitative scales.

In my view, the hybrid system was a noble experiment, but the evidence for it was insufficient. I will be happy to change my mind if more data come in to support this proposal. A scientific committee appointed by the American Psychiatric Association also concluded that the proposal had not been sufficiently validated. In the end, radical changes in classification require strong evidence. Thus, in December 2012, it was decided to repeat the *DSM–IV* criteria for PDs, word for word, in *DSM–5*. Although the alternative system was consigned to Section III of the published manual, several members of the work group are promoting the rejected model. It remains to be seen whether further research will interest practitioners in using this system. Furthermore, because preparation of the sixth edition of the *DSM* could take another 15 years, the ultimate fate of this proposal remains uncertain.

The only substantive change for PD classification in *DSM–5* was the demise of the five-axis system introduced in *DSM–III;* one can no longer speak of disorders as being "on Axis II." In *DSM–5*, all diagnoses are made on a single axis. This is an important and positive development. Putting PD diagnoses on a separate axis never succeeded in giving them more attention and, if anything, provided another reason to ignore them. (How many times have you seen a diagnosis of "Axis II, deferred"?)

Finally, a diagnostic system that is too complex could have hurt patients with PDs by discouraging busy clinicians from recognizing them—on top of an already strong reluctance. This is why some researchers viewed the rejection of the hybrid proposal with palpable relief (Black, 2013b). As Zimmerman (2012) pointed out, even if the current system is bad, one should not make radical changes without strong evidence. My greatest concern was that the people who would have most been hurt by this system would have been the patients who most need our help.

THE FUTURE OF PD DIAGNOSIS

The current categorical system for PDs is nothing to be proud of, but *DSM–5* has retained it, so this is the way that PDs will continue to be diagnosed for some time to come. The "paradigm shift" in classification that Kupfer and Regier (2011) had hoped for, in which all categories of mental illness would eventually be replaced by dimensional scoring, is a dead letter for now. Finally, the belief that quantitative measures drawn from factor analysis of self-report data might correspond to biomarkers that could be identified by neurobiological research remains just that—a belief.

However, a dimensional model has also been proposed for the World Health Organization (WHO), which will be publishing the 11th edition of the *International Classification of Diseases (ICD–11)* by 2017. This system (Tyrer, Crawford, Mulder, & the *ICD–11* Working Group for the Revision of Classification of Personality Disorders, 2011) has one great advantage: It is rather simple. Clinicians would be asked to rate patients on a scale of 5 points: no PD, personality difficulty, PD, complex PD, and severe PD. There would be no specific categories, although clinicians would also be asked to score patients on five trait domains: asocial, dissocial (i.e., antisocial), anankastic (i.e., obsessional), anxious–dependent, and emotionally unstable.

Assuming that WHO accepts this system, we could have two competing and incompatible systems for PD classification. I have the same concern about *ICD–11* as about the hybrid system: Can clinicians be trained to make reliable and valid ratings of trait profiles? Even with a simpler system, they would need a lot of training, which would in turn be expensive.

A much more radical (but also more complex) proposal to eliminate categorical diagnosis in psychiatry entirely has been promoted by the National Institute of Mental Health (NIMH). Thomas Insel, the director of the NIMH, has proposed a system to replace *DSM* called Research Domain Criteria (RDoC; Insel et al., 2010). This model is already being applied to the assessment of research grants. RDoC is a matrix of theoretical dimensions of psychopathology across many levels of analysis. It is based on the idea that mental illnesses fall along a spectrum and that quantitative measures will shed light on the endophenotypes underlying mental disorders.

The RDoC system attempts to eliminate all categories of mental illness in favor of scoring procedures believed to correspond more closely to neurobiology. Although some consider it the wave of the future, at our present state of knowledge, it is overambitious. Mental health practitioners will continue to use *DSM* diagnoses because they are familiar ways to allow communication; practitioners would have to be convinced that alternatives are scientifically or clinically superior.

RDoC would not just dimensionalize PD but make it disappear completely, in favor of ratings of variations in cognition, emotion, and behavior. In my opinion, the RDoC matrix is, at this point, full of holes where solid research should be. Furthermore, this ideological proposal comes from an NIMH director who is on record as wanting to abolish psychiatry by combining it with neurology (Insel & Quirion, 2005). RDoC are a manifesto for neurobiology that also takes little or no account of psychology, effectively dismissing any research not based on, or linked to neurochemistry, neurophysiology, or brain imaging. The idea that mental disorders are brain disorders goes along with the mindless reductionism of contemporary psychiatry (Paris, 2008b).

The construct of a PD will survive this onslaught. Clinical psychologists, social workers, and psychiatrists work with real people and do not spend their time in laboratories. They are not ready to reject the concept of mind or view a person as a neural network. For better or for worse, our current PD categories are associated with a personological approach, consistent with the practice of psychotherapy.

A LOST OPPORTUNITY

The failure to revise procedures for PD diagnosis in *DSM–5* was in many ways a lost opportunity. We still need a better general definition of PD, even if the hybrid system produced one that was too complicated. Another loss was the need to repair flaws in the criteria for specific PDs. After 20 years of additional research, the work group might have come up with a better set of algorithms than those found in *DSM–IV*. The current criteria continue to be sorely deficient in discriminant function, which is why patients who meet criteria for one PD will often meet criteria for others. Moreover, some of the categories in *DSM–5* are next to useless because they describe a single trait.

The most serious loss concerned patients who fit the general description of a PD but do not meet criteria for any of the 10 categories listed. They still have to be diagnosed as "personality disorder, unspecified," with about half of those who meet overall PD criteria falling into this group (Zimmerman, Rothschild, & Chelminski, 2005). The fact that the most frequent diagnosis in practice cannot be specified is a serious indictment of the current system. A better description of trait profiles in patients with this diagnosis would have allowed a vague category to be replaced with a more precise assessment of the traits that characterize individual patients, but I cannot recommend going to Section III of the manual to do so.

A 2013 issue of the journal *Personality Disorders: Theory, Research, and Treatment* presented a series of target papers and commentaries that reviewed the story of *DSM–5*'s approach to PDs. The most sensible, in my view, was a paper by Tom Widiger (a prominent player in the *DSM–IV* process who was not consulted about *DSM–5*). Widiger (2013) pointed out that it was a mistake to create a new and untested system when the FFM was already available and could have been applied for clinical use. Widiger was in favor of retaining some categories and noted that no one had ever taken the trouble to check out the discriminant validity of their diagnostic criteria, almost all of which could have been improved.

One does not need to be a psychometrician to understand that a system with problems like those of the *DSM* badly needed revision. One might conclude that being stuck with the same system as in previous editions is dispiriting. Yet despite all the research in recent decades, none of the proposed alternatives was sufficiently better than the status quo to gain wide support. It should be kept in mind, however, that the situation for PD diagnosis is not much worse than any of the other groupings in *DSM–5*. Until we know much more about mental disorders, any attempt to develop a scientific classification is premature and bound to fail.

I support Widiger's views for two reasons. First, they would allow a degree of continuity for research communities studying well-investigated categories such as BPD and ASPD. Second, adapting the FFM for clinical use, most probably using a brief self-report instrument, would be superior to developing a new and untested system.

In summary, PDs as a whole do not quite fit with either classical trait psychology or a categorical medical model. The current categories of PD are problematic and can only be regarded as provisional. Eventually, when we know a good deal more about their endophenotypes, they will be replaced. For now, there may be value in retaining some categories that are familiar to clinicians and that have a strong basis in research. However, given the passion that has marked the categorical versus dimensional controversy, I cannot be optimistic that these principles will be adopted any time soon.

3

Etiology

In this chapter, I develop a general theory on the etiology of PDs. I propose that only interactions among biological temperament, psychological adversities, and social factors are sufficient conditions for the development of this form of psychopathology.

TEMPERAMENT

Every child has a unique temperament. Heritability accounts for about half the variance in traits that eventually emerge and also determines the type of PD that can develop (Paris, 1998). Although an abnormal temperament need not by itself lead to a PD, it can be a risk factor for psychopathology.

Almost 30 years ago, the great British child psychiatrist Michael Rutter (1987) wrote a classic and seminal paper describing the hierarchical relationship among temperament, traits, and PDs. In this model, personality

http://dx.doi.org/10.1037/14642-004
A Concise Guide to Personality Disorders, by J. Paris

is rooted in temperament (heritable biological factors producing individual differences in emotion, cognition, and behavior). Personality traits (stable characteristics of emotion, cognition, and behavior) are amalgams of temperament and life experience, and disorders are pathological exaggerations of traits.

Temperament, although present at birth, is difficult to measure directly. Researchers have studied infant behavior, measuring differences on dimensions of positive affect, fear, frustration or anger, and effortful control (Rothbart, 2007). However, there is a paucity of research in which children with problematic temperaments have been followed into adulthood to determine the risk for PD or other mental disorders. Kagan (2012) followed a cohort of infants with behavioral inhibition, a likely precursor of anxious PDs, but only into adolescence. Published long-term follow-ups have usually started in middle childhood, although some have followed their subjects for decades (Caspi & Roberts, 1999; Cohen, Crawford, Johnson, & Kasen, 2005; Tremblay, 2006). These studies did not measure early temperament, however. Moreover, birth cohort studies that have followed subjects from "the cradle to the grave" do not have a high enough rate of severe psychopathology in adulthood to produce that kind of data.

Another problem is the absence of biological markers associated with temperamental variations (Rettew & McKee, 2005). Given the strong evidence for heritability of personality traits (Plomin, DeFries, Knopik, & Neiderhiser, 2012), one might expect to find such relationships, but researchers will need many decades to correlate the enormous complexity of brain structure and function with temperament. It is unlikely that advances in brain chemistry or connectivity will be able to address this problem in the foreseeable future.

PERSONALITY TRAITS

Personality traits are an amalgam of temperament and life experience, and thus they reflect the effects of interactions between inborn tendencies and the psychosocial environment (M. Rutter, 1987). Most have a heritability close to 0.5, are reasonably stable by late childhood, and remain fairly stable over the life course (Widiger & Costa, 2013). This is not to say that personality cannot change but that traits set limits on the extent of change.

The stability of traits is an important observation for the practice of psychotherapy. We cannot change personality, but we can help patients to function better using traits more effectively (Paris, 1998). For example, although introverts may always remain shy, there are ways, particularly in an age of computers, to use that trait adaptively. Similarly, neuroticism can be adaptive if associated with emotional responsiveness rather than with pathology, particularly when people learn how to control their emotions (Gross, 2013).

The widely believed principle that the quality of parenting shapes personality traits is partly right and partly wrong. There are statistical relationships between poor parenting and outcome, as well as clear-cut negative effects from abuse and neglect, but these risks do not predictably or necessarily produce major psychopathology in adulthood (Fergusson & Mullen, 1999; M. Rutter & Rutter, 1993).

By and large, it is easier to ruin a child than to raise one. Many books have been written about the right and wrong way to be a parent. Yet most children develop in their own way, based on their temperamental characteristics. Moreover, the impact of the psychosocial environment is itself genetically mediated (Belsky & Pluess, 2013)—that is, people with different temperaments respond to the same environmental events in unique ways. For example, those who are environmentally sensitive (i.e., highly neurotic) are influenced more by both positive and negative life events, benefiting from a good environment more than those who are relatively insensitive (Belsky & Pluess, 2009). Moreover, positive temperamental characteristics lead to gene–environment interactions that help explain high levels of resilience to traumatic events during childhood (M. Rutter, 2012).

A great deal of effort has gone into the precise measurement of personality traits. Researchers almost always use self-report questionnaires with established reliability and external validity and in which trait domains are identified by factor analysis. The most widely used instruments are based on the five-factor model (FFM), a theory of personality that describes five broad domains (see Chapters 1 and 2, this volume). The main limitation of the FFM is that it depends on self-report. People are not always accurate when reporting negative traits so questionnaires should ideally be supplemented by direct observations, peer ratings, and (eventually) biomarkers (Kagan, 2012). Nonetheless, given the problems of clinical ratings, self-report remains the most empirically validated option.

Another limitation is that the traits identified in community samples do not account for all features of severe psychopathology. As discussed in Chapter 2, there are several alternatives to the FFM that have specifically set out to measure behavioral patterns seen in clinical settings.

Yet however traits are measured, heritability always accounts for nearly half the variance (Plomin, DeFries, Knopik, & Neiderhiser, 2012). The method most often used to quantify heritability is *behavioral genetics*, in which monozygotic (MZ) and dizygotic (DZ) twins can be compared for concordance in diagnosis or in trait dimensions. A trait can be determined to be heritable to the extent that concordance is higher in MZ than in DZ twins. Other methods, such as adoption studies, or studies of twins separated at birth, are not often practical but yield similar results.

Behavioral genetic methods also yield an estimate of environmental influence, which accounts for the other half of the variance (Plomin et al., 2012). Children who grow up in the same family are no more similar than perfect strangers (Dunn & Plomin, 1990). Thus, the environmental variance in personality is not shared (i.e., the result of being brought up in a particular family), as past theories would have predicted. Instead, it is almost entirely unshared (i.e., affected by environmental factors outside the family or by unique experiences within a family). This finding, which overturns many long-held assumptions of developmental psychology, has been one of the biggest surprises in psychological research over the past 50 years.

It would be useful to find biomarkers associated with personality traits—either the broad dimensions of the FFM or its more narrowly defined facets—but no such relationships have been found. There is some evidence that abnormalities in serotonin activity correlate with a tendency to be impulsive (Siever & Davis, 1991), yet even that relationship is not consistent (Carver & Miller, 2006). Although establishing biomarkers has to be a goal for further research, in the current state of knowledge, neuro-scientists don't know what to look for. Trait dimensions as currently defined are consistent, but they may or may not be biological constructs.

BIOLOGICAL FACTORS IN PDs

We know that PDs are at least partially heritable. What we do not know is how genes shape the brains of people who develop such disorders. The heritability of PDs has been demonstrated by a series of studies, almost all of which were conducted in Scandinavia (Kendler et al., 2008; Reichborn-Kjennerud et al., 2013; Torgersen, Kringlen, & Cramer, 2001). The level of heritability is in the same range as traits, about half the variance for most disorders. Borderline PD (BPD), long thought to be an environmental con-dition, has a single heritable factor that accounts for 55% of the variance in all nine *Diagnostic and Statistical Manual of Mental Disorders* (5th ed.; *DSM–5*; American Psychiatric Association, 2013) criteria (Reichborn-Kjennerud et al., 2013). These findings overturn a good deal of conven-tional wisdom. Yet despite intensive research, no biomarkers for any type of PD have been discovered. Researchers should not feel apologetic, however; there are no biomarkers for any major mental disorder (Hyman, 2010).

What heritability determines is not PD itself but who is and who is not vulnerable to PD. A vulnerable temperament makes the development of a PD more likely, but this outcome can only be explained by complex interactions between traits and environmental stressors (Paris, 1998).

Temperament also determines the type of PD that can develop in any person. A highly introverted person will not develop narcissistic PD, and a highly extraverted person will not develop avoidant PD. In this way, genes "bend the twig" but do not determine the shape of the tree. Also, the specific symptoms associated with severe PDs, such as BPD, may not have the same heritable component as the traits that underlie the disorder. This additional complexity is why some PDs, contrary to theory, are only partially continu-ous with the domains of personality.

Finally, the idea that heritability means that traits cannot change is mistaken (M. Rutter, 2006). In fact, some of the most important effects of heritable factors in psychopathology lie in individual differences in susceptibility to environmental risks (Rutter, 2006). Some people are highly resilient and are surprisingly unaffected by serious adversities in life. Others are highly sensitive and are affected by all kinds of life events, good or bad (Belsky & Pluess, 2013).

In summary, biological factors in PDs can only be understood in terms of gene–environment interactions. Nonetheless, it would be useful if we could identify biomarkers associated with these conditions. This would help to make diagnosis precise. It might also open up the possibility of defining high-risk populations are most likely to develop PDs. Finally, biomarkers would be useful in research.

Potential biomarkers for PDs could include abnormalities in genetic variations, neurotransmission, neuropsychological measures, or neuroimaging (volume, activity, and connectivity of specific brain areas). There is a fairly large body of research examining each of these strategies in major mental disorders. Almost all of the research on PDs has focused on the borderline category.

Although this literature is large, the state of current knowledge, as described in a number of review articles (Mauchnik & Schmahl, 2010; New, Goodman, Triebwasser, & Siever, 2008; Ruocco, 2005), can be summarized as follows:

1. No specific allele has been found that can account for any PD, and those that have been studied in BPD account for no more than 1% of the variance (e.g., Ni, Chan, Chan, McMain, & Kennedy, 2009). It is likely that heritability is associated with the activity of a large number of interacting genes.
2. There is no evidence for chemical imbalances in PDs. There is some evidence that abnormal serotonin activity is associated with impulsivity (New et al., 2008), but this finding is neither fully consistent nor specific to any diagnosis or trait profile.
3. Neuropsychological testing shows that impulsive PDs are associated with a failure of higher centers (prefrontal cortex) to inhibit impulses and emotions coming from the limbic system and the amygdala (Ruocco, 2005).

4. Neuroimaging studies in patients with BPD show decreased activity in prefrontal cortex (Mauchnik & Schmahl, 2010), reduced volume in the amygdala and hippocampus (Ruocco, Amirthavasagam, & Zakzanis, 2012), an overactivity of "alarm" circuits in the amygdala (Donegan et al., 2003), associated with a failure of cortical inhibition (Koenigsberg et al., 2014). These findings are interesting but do not go much beyond what we already know through clinical observation.

At this point biological findings in PD can be understood as first steps in a long journey toward understanding how the mental abnormalities in PD are reflected in the brain. Moreover, none of these results is strong enough to justify any specific biological treatment.

PSYCHOLOGICAL FACTORS

We have a lot to learn about the role of the psychological environment in PD, and what we thought we knew is in doubt. It was long believed that PD is the direct result of an unhappy childhood. These ideas have been associated with psychoanalysis. It was also assumed that the more severe the disorder, the more likely it had its origins in the earliest stages of development—a theory so ubiquitous that prominent PD researchers have taken it for granted (Millon & Davis, 2011). These ideas have also had a vast influence on psychotherapy, encouraging clinicians to search for past traumas to account for present distress.

Yet the idea that the cause of PD lies in childhood is oversimplistic. It has a grain of truth in that early adversity is, statistically speaking, a risk factor for psychopathology (Rutter & Rutter, 1993). Yet most people with unhappy childhoods develop no mental disorder at all (Rutter, 2012). Resilience is not the exception, but the rule. Moreover, only some patients with mental disorders report psychological trauma as children (Paris, 2000). Although some experiences are particularly traumatic, even people with a history of childhood sexual abuse (CSA) do not necessarily suffer major sequelae (Fergusson & Mullen, 1999). PD is the outcome of complex interactions that we are only beginning to understand.

It follows that practitioners who routinely attribute adult psychopathology to childhood experiences are making a cognitive error. They are confusing correlation with causation. For every patient who comes in with symptoms associated with a history of adversity, there are thousands of others who are functioning reasonably well and will never seek clinical attention. There are also people who have such an abnormal temperament that they are at risk for PD without having experienced severe childhood adversity. Nonetheless, because people who do develop severe PDs are more likely to have had adverse childhood experiences, particularly in the borderline (Paris, 2008a) and antisocial categories (Robins, 1966), clinicians still need to explore these histories carefully.

These relationships are best framed in terms of gene–environment interactions. Doing so can be difficult. We prefer simple explanations to complex ones. From childhood on, our minds see cause and effect in everything, even when there is no relationship (Bloom, 2013). We have to be trained to think multivariately, even if it is a strain to keep that perspective in mind.

Those patients with PD who have had a reasonably normal childhood may have had special needs, based on abnormal temperament, that are hard for any family to meet. In adulthood, they may therefore perceive their upbringing as inadequate. As Dobbs (2009) suggested, some people are "orchids" (successful only in just the right environment), and others are "dandelions" (able to cope with almost any environment). This point of view is also consistent with the research of Belsky and Pluess (2013), which shows strong variations in environmental sensitivity, such that people who are sensitive to adversity also benefit more than most others from a positive environment. This is a hopeful message for clinicians who treat PD.

CHILDHOOD ADVERSITY IN BPD

Strong evidence for environmental risk factors in PDs has come from studies of BPD. CSA is common in this disorder and, when present, makes its course more severe (Soloff, Lynch, & Kelly, 2002). Although about two thirds of patients with BPD report some form of CSA, these large numbers are misleading. This is because they include events that do not lead to sequelae in normal populations (Paris, 2008a). Thus, single incidents with strangers or nonrelatives, not involving physical contact, are not risk factors for any mental disorder. However, severe abuse, perpetrated by family members or caretakers, can lead to psychopathology (Fergusson & Mullen, 1999). The parameters of CSA (perpetrator, nature of the act, duration) are more important than its simple presence in a patient's history (Paris, 2008a).

Severe childhood abuse of any kind occurs in only about a third of BPD cases, with abuse from a caretaker in about a quarter of these patients (Zanarini, 2000). This finding points to risk, but clinicians should not assume that every patient with BPD must have been abused as a child. The disorder is a final common pathway, demonstrating what Cicchetti and Rogosch (1996) called "equifinality" (the same outcome arising from different causes). Different patients also receive different doses of adversity that have different consequences (Paris, 2008a). Some BPD patients have histories of severe child abuse that go a long way to explaining the severity of their symptoms. Others have only mild or intermittent abuse that should be seen as part of a larger picture of family dysfunction. Finally, about a third have never experienced abuse at all.

The most important parameters of CSA are the relationship to the perpetrator and the nature of the sexual contact. The most pathogenic form of CSA is parental incest (Finkelhor, Ormrod, Turner, & Hamby, 2005), but it is not the most common form of CSA reported by BPD patients. It more frequent to hear that stepfathers, boyfriends of the mother, or older brothers were perpetrators (Paris, 2008a).

The term *abuse* can sometimes be abused. It is used to describe all sorts of things that can go wrong in childhood. Physical abuse is clearer and is another common risk factor for BPD, although not as specific to the disorder as CSA. Researchers have also studied emotional abuse, that is, constant and hurtful criticism from caretakers, which is frequently reported (Zanarini, 2000).

These adversities are more common in dysfunctional families. In most ways, a chaotic and dysfunctional family is a more essential risk factor, and a more important focus for clinical attention, than any specific type of adversity. Parents of patients with BPD can have serious psychopathology, including substance abuse, depression, and PDs (White, Gunderson, Zanarini, & Hudson, 2003). This does not make them ideal caretakers for vulnerable children.

When BPD develops in the absence of trauma, the failure of parents to understand children with special emotional needs may be important. Linehan (1993) conceptualized BPD as an interaction between a vulnerable temperament (emotion dysregulation) and the failure of parents to understand the problem (an invalidating environment). A good body of research has supported this seminal idea, and later chapters in this book examine its clinical implications.

Parker (1983) developed a self-report instrument, the Parental Bonding Index (PBI), based on a more general theory about what makes for successful parenting. The essential idea is that children need emotional warmth and empathy, as well as a respect for their autonomy. These dimensions tend to be orthogonal and can be measured (for each parent) by subscales of the PBI. Parker's most consistent finding was that depression is associated with "affectionless control" (low affection combined with overprotection). Our own research group found similar results in BPD using the PBI to study recollections of parenting, compared with patients without a PD (Zweig-Frank & Paris, 1991) and to patients who had other types of PD (Paris, Zweig-Frank, & Guzder, 1994a). The results also suggested that BPD patients can suffer from *biparental failure*, that is, the absence of validating responses from either parent.

Again, interactions between temperament and adversity are the key to understanding these pathways. A good example came from a research study (Laporte, Paris, Guttman, & Russell, 2011) designed by my colleague Lise Laporte. We studied 56 pairs of sisters in which one had BPD and observed that concordance for the disorder only occurred in three of these pairs. This finding was particularly striking because we had a sample of severely ill patients, and both sisters had been exposed to the same traumatic events (Laporte, Paris, Russell, Guttman, & Correa, 2012). However, when we gave sisters a measure of personality traits developed for research on clinical populations (Livesley, Jang, & Vernon, 1998), differences were dramatic: BPD probands had abnormal scores on every subscale, whereas the normal sisters did not. Our interpretation was that trauma and adversity are most likely to be associated with BPD in children with an abnormal temperament.

The research on antisocial PD (ASPD) is less well-developed but shows a number of similarities to findings in BPD. It has been known for decades that dysfunctional families, particularly those in which the father is also antisocial, are also strong risk factors for the disorder (Robins, 1966). The risks are essentially the same as for conduct disorder, an early form of antisociality in young children and a required antecedent for making the diagnosis in adults. Most likely, ASPD is the result of an adverse environment in children with an abnormal temperament.

Research about environmental risk factors in other PDs is too thin to reach any firm conclusions, but a similar model might be applied. Interactions between temperament and adversity is a general principle for understanding the origins of psychopathology, and it will guide much of the rest of this book.

SOCIAL FACTORS IN PDs

One of the main mechanisms behind resilience to adversity is access to social support and to attachments that lie beyond the family (Rutter, 2012). Moreover, because PD involves a disjunction between personality and social demands, the risk for developing these disorders depends on social context. Traits that are adaptive in one society can be maladaptive in another. When social demands change over time, the risk for developing a PD can also change.

A good example is ASPD, which has a high prevalence in developed countries—about 3% in North America (Robins & Regier, 1991). In contrast, there is a low prevalence in traditional societies, such as Taiwan (Hwu, Yeh, & Chang, 1989). ASPD increased in prevalence in the United States and Europe after the Second World War, and these cohort effects may have been associated with the social and family breakdown that marked those decades (Rutter & Smith, 1995). Thus social risk factors operate through two mechanisms: They further aggravate psychological risk, and they interfere with resilience factors that could be based on a supportive social environment.

It has been suggested that BPD has also increased in prevalence since the Second World War (Millon, 1993). It is certainly surprising that this important disorder was never described before 1937. I have long wondered why people in the past, who could also have had a difficult temperament and who could also have been exposed to psychosocial adversity, did not develop BPD. Yet although most severe mental disorders can be recognized throughout history, one does not read about people cutting themselves and taking recurrent overdoses until about 75 years ago. The explanation may be that patients with the same underlying traits presented in different ways in other historical periods (Paris & Lis, 2013).

Narcissistic PD is another disorder that may be socially sensitive. It has been suggested that trait narcissism has increased over the past several decades, largely due to a more indulgent style of parenting and a society that values self-esteem about achievement (Twenge, 2011). This intriguing hypothesis requires more research.

Finally, it is possible that PDs in general are on the increase because of the rapid social change associated with modernity over the globe (Paris, 2014a). The type of PD one develops would be determined by temperament, but whether one's traits become amplified to the level of disorder would be influenced by the social environment.

DEVELOPING AN INTEGRATED MODEL

Let us now consider an integrated etiological model of PD that takes into account all these risk factors: biological, psychological, and social. The biological risks involve a difficult temperament, which could be impulsive and extraverted or anxious and introverted. Although children could also have other combinations of temperamental variables, these are the two basic dimensions of psychopathology in children: *externalizing* and *internalizing* (Achenbach & Ndetei, 2012). A distinction between symptoms associated with impulsive actions versus symptoms associated with inner suffering is supported by a large body of research (Achenbach & Ndetei, 2012).

Temperamental risks also lead to higher environmental risks. For example, children with an externalizing temperament are more likely to come into conflict with parents, peers, and teachers (Rutter & Rutter, 1993). In a family where other children have a different trait profile, temperamentally vulnerable children may be scapegoated. On the other hand, good parenting can help children with a difficult temperament overcome many difficulties. What is needed is high structure, predictable expectations, and empathy (Gordon, 2000). In contrast, a pattern of inconsistent, disruptive parenting with insufficient monitoring is characteristic of parents with conduct-disordered children (Berg-Nielsen, Vikan, & Dahl, 2002).

Similarly, parental behaviors have a relationship to the development of internalizing symptoms. Affectionless control is a risk factor for depression and anxiety in children (Berg-Nielsen et al., 2002), and there is evidence that this style of parenting is related to all disorders in which anxiety is prominent (Parker, 1983). Conversely, sensitive parenting can help children overcome internalizing temperamental patterns and become healthily introverted adults.

The social environment plays a role in buffering the influence of temperament and parenting on personality. Living in a good neighborhood, going to a good school, and having access to community activities are all important factors in the development of a healthy personality. Conversely, bad neighborhoods, bad schools, and living in a socially disintegrated community will be risk factors for psychopathology (Rutter & Rutter, 1993). These risks will have more negative effects on those who are temperamentally vulnerable as well as on those who come from dysfunctional families. Social factors may be of particular importance in adolescence, when problematic traits can interfere with the developmental task of identity formation. We live in a society where each person has to find his or her own role and niche in society, and this may be more difficult for those who are temperamentally impulsive or unusually anxious (Paris, 2014a).

In summary, PDs are most likely to develop when all of these factors, interacting with each other, are present. No single risk factor is sufficient to produce a PD.

4

Prevalence, Precursors, and Outcome

This chapter reviews research on the prevalence of personality disorders (PDs) in the community, childhood precursors of PDs, and clinically important research on PD outcome.

EPIDEMIOLOGICAL STUDIES

Epidemiological research on the community prevalence of PDs was rare until fairly recently. Researchers were unsure whether these complex conditions could be reliably identified in large-scale surveys.

The first extensive project in the United States to examine the prevalence of the major mental disorders listed in the third edition of the *Diagnostic and Statistical Manual of Mental Disorders* (*DSM–III*) was the Epidemiological Catchment Area (ECA) study (Robins & Regier, 1991). However, the ECA only examined antisocial PD (ASPD), considered to be

http://dx.doi.org/10.1037/14642-005
A Concise Guide to Personality Disorders, by J. Paris

the one category that was defined well enough to be assessed in a community sample.

Over the past two decades, the situation has changed greatly. A major study conducted in Norway (Torgersen et al., 2001) examined all the PDs in the manual. The findings showed that PDs, as defined by *DSM–III*, are common, with at least 10% of the community population meeting criteria for one category or another. A second study, conducted in the United Kingdom and based on criteria from the fourth edition of the *DSM* (*DSM–IV;* Coid, Yang, Tyrer, Roberts, & Ullrich, 2006), came up with similar results. A third study, also based on *DSM–IV* and drawing on data from the large-scale National Comorbidity Study (NCS) in the United States (Lenzenweger, Lane, Loranger, & Kessler, 2007), came up with similar levels of prevalence.

Thus, a consensus has emerged that about one in 10 people meet criteria for a PD. In these studies, ASPD was found to be particularly frequent, with a prevalence of approximately 2% to 3%. Borderline PD (BPD) was less frequent, with rates ranging between something less than 1% and 2% (Paris, 2010a). However, all these numbers depend on the definitions in the *DSM*—if a higher bar had been set, prevalence could have easily have been halved.

Epidemiological research is usually more likely to overestimate prevalence than to underestimate it. In a survey of alcohol and drug abuse in the United States, the National Epidemiologic Survey on Alcohol and Related Conditions (NESARC; Grant et al., 2004) results differed dramatically from previous studies. NESARC had one big advantage: access to a particularly large sample. However, its estimates of prevalence seem to have been inflated by the use of too low a bar for diagnosis. The study found that as many as 15% to 20% of the population could meet criteria for one or more PD diagnoses. A reanalysis of the same data (Trull, Jahng, Tomko, Wood, & Sher, 2010), raising the bar for formal diagnosis, found that although the prevalence of PDs was still high, rates were much closer to what the earlier studies had found. Unfortunately, the higher numbers have been quoted ever since. This may reflect bias and self-interest. When researchers write grants or introductory sections of papers submitted for publication, they usually aim to prove that the problem under study is common in the community.

The lack of a clear boundary between PD and trait variation remains the real problem, and it is not easily solved. In the end, prevalence depends on the judgment of investigators who measure it (Paris, 2010a). For example, Grant et al. (2004) claimed that obsessive–compulsive PD has a community prevalence of 7%. This is an enormous number, dwarfing the prevalence of common disorders such as depression. Yet because obsessive–compulsive PD is an almost pure trait disorder, it is not at all clear that everyone who met criteria in this study had a mental illness. Perhaps all it tells us is that 7% of the population is more perfectionistic than is good for them.

By contrast, PDs are common in clinical settings. Zimmerman, Rothschild, and Chelminski (2005) estimated that up to half of all outpatients meet criteria for one category or another. The irony is that clinicians who had a clinical focus on mood and anxiety missed many PD diagnoses. In particular, patients with BPD were often diagnosed with bipolar disorder because they have mood swings, even when they have never had episodes of mania or hypomania (Paris, Gunderson, & Weinberg, 2007).

The clinic is where we should be sharpening our diagnostic skills, not in community populations where most people manage without any treatment. The failure to recognize PDs in these settings is one of the great tragedies of our time. Patients are being managed with interventions designed for anxiety or depression, and their personality pathology may not be addressed at all.

Another problem is that a continuous relationship between traits and disorders makes it difficult to determine cutoff points. This may explain why many estimates of PD prevalence in the general population have ranged as high as 10% (Paris, 2010a). In the largest study, obsessive–compulsive PD had the highest prevalence, even though this diagnosis fades imperceptibly into normality. In contrast, the prevalence of BPD, which has more symptoms that are distinct from normality, was much lower, similar to that found for major mental disorders such as schizophrenia (Paris, 2010a).

CHILDHOOD PRECURSORS OF PDs

A large body of recent research has examined the precursors of PD in childhood (De Fruyt & De Clercq, 2014; Scott, Stepp, & Pilkonis, 2014; Tackett, Herzhoff, Reardon, De Clercq, & Sharp, 2014; Tackett & Sharp, 2014). If PDs are rooted in temperamental variation, one would expect them to be apparent in childhood. This sequence has been well documented in ASPD. Follow-up research (Robins, 1966) indicated that early-onset conduct disorder almost always precedes ASPD. In fact, it is the same disorder but at different stages of development. The main caveat is that not every child with conduct disorder ends up developing ASPD (Zoccolillo, Pickles, Quinton, & Rutter, 1992).

It has been accepted in all the *DSM* manuals since the third edition that one cannot even make an ASPD diagnosis without a childhood history of conduct disorder. This is one of the few examples in which a research finding has actually changed diagnostic criteria. Moreover, the earlier and more severe conduct symptoms are, the more likely the outcome will be ASPD (Zoccolillo et al., 1992). In a longitudinal community study (Caspi & Roberts, 1999), antisocial behavior at age 18 could be predicted with surprising accuracy by a 90-minute interview of mother and child conducted at age 3.

It would be helpful if we knew as much about the precursors of BPD as we do about ASPD. BPD usually begins in adolescence, a stage at which all its clinical features are already apparent (Chanen & McCutcheon, 2013). The idea that the disorder should not be diagnosed at that stage is plain wrong. It is based on the idea that adolescents grow out of problems like this, but they don't. Even so, the fifth edition of the *DSM* wisely advises clinicians to ensure that PD symptoms have been present for at least a year.

What are BPD patients like before adolescence? Although many patients report an unhappy childhood, they may or may not have had observable symptoms before puberty. If they do, the clinical presentation may be different. Research is just beginning to address this question. The most consistent finding is that children who later develop BPD have a mixture of internalizing and externalizing symptomatology.

This principle was illustrated by the Pittsburgh Girls Study, a longitudinal follow-up of a high-risk group (Stepp, Pilkonis, Hipwell, Loeber, & Stouthamer-Loeber, 2010). The researchers found that externalizing disorders (attention-deficit/hyperactivity disorder, conduct disorder, and oppositional defiant disorder) as well as internalizing disorders (particularly posttraumatic stress disorder) tend to precede BPD in the childhood of women who develop symptoms in adolescence. It should be kept in mind, however, that there are multiple pathways to BPD, so that no single profile predicts the outcome (in the way that conduct disorder predicts ASPD).

An ongoing longitudinal study of prepubertal girls with symptoms resembling BPD (Zanarini et al., 2011) found similar psychosocial risk factors at age 11 to those documented in adults: abuse, neglect, and dysfunctional families. When these cohorts are followed up into adulthood, the study could provide further insight into the precursors of BPD in adolescence and adulthood.

In a study of 12-year-olds from a birth cohort, Belsky et al. (2012) identified a group with BPD features. The findings were that BPD characteristics are heritable but that children with these features also had a history of trauma and family dysfunction. This is further confirmation of the importance of gene–environment interactions.

My research group studied a group of prepubertal children in a day program who had symptoms resembling adult BPD and whom we followed into adolescence (Zelkowitz et al., 2007). We also found risk factors similar to adult BPD (Guzder, Paris, Zelkowitz, & Marchessault, 1996). However, most of our cases were male, and although these men continued to have life problems, they did not develop BPD over time.

The ideal study of childhood precursors of PD would need to follow large cohorts into adulthood. This has only rarely been carried out, largely because of the expense. The Children in the Community Study (Cohen, Crawford, Johnson, & Kasen, 2005) attempted to do so by following a group of children in the Albany–Saratoga area of New York State over the course of 30 years. However, due in part to attrition, they were not able to identify enough cases that met full PD criteria and so could only report predictors of PD symptoms, limiting the generalizability of the findings to subclinical populations.

In summary, there is evidence that BPD has precursors before puberty, but they may or may not come to clinical attention. Over the next 10 years, as longitudinal data come in, we should know more.

Much less is known about the childhood precursors of other PDs. A long-term study (Kagan, 2004) of infants with "behavioral inhibition" (high social anxiety) during infancy could have shed light on the antecedents of avoidant PD, marked by social anxiety and withdrawal. Most of Kagan's (2004) subjects did well in adolescence, but some continued to have symptoms. Unfortunately the follow-up did not last long enough to determine which diagnoses developed in the adult years.

OUTCOME

PDs used to be thought of as chronic, lifelong, and hopeless conditions. This perception has been an important factor in the reluctance of clinicians to diagnose or treat them. However, long-term follow-up research has shown that most patients get better with time. The prognosis is actually better than for many other mental disorders.

Clinicians tend to overestimate chronicity mainly because patients who continue to have symptoms keep coming for help, whereas those who have no longer have symptoms do not. This is what Cohen and Cohen (1984) called the "clinician's illusion." You won't often see recovered patients in your office unless you have arranged for long-term follow-up. Moreover, the unfairly negative image of PD outcome is shaped by the cases that do not do well. Meanwhile, new patients who have not yet recovered, as well as the important minority of patients who fail to recover, continue to flood our clinics.

Moreover, as shown by Zimmerman and Mattia (1999), many patients are misdiagnosed and treated either with medication or standard therapy for their "comorbid" mood disorders. It is only when these conditions fail to respond that a PD diagnosis is even considered.

Twenty-five years ago, a group of retrospective studies following BPD patients into middle age showed a striking pattern of recovery after 15 years. This finding came as a surprise, but perhaps we could have anticipated it.

Many of us had wondered why most of our patients were young, and why older patients were notable in their absence. It was hard to believe they had all died by suicide or from illness.

These studies of 15-year outcome were published in the 1980s. Two were conducted in private hospitals (McGlashan, 1986; Plakun, Burkhardt, & Muller, 1985), one in a state hospital (Stone, 1990), and one in a general hospital (Paris, Brown, & Nowlis, 1987). Despite differences in samples, attrition levels, and methodologies, the results were almost identical. By age 40, most patients were functioning better, and the majority were no longer in treatment.

A few years later, a long-term study in Iowa (Black, Baumgard, & Bell, 1995) reported similar findings for patients with ASPD, some of whom were followed for decades. They showed gradual improvement over time but continued to have difficulties. What BPD and ASPD have in common is impulsivity. It is known that most disorders characterized by this trait (substance abuse, bulimia nervosa) improve over time. In fact, most people are less impulsive at 40 than they were at 20. These changes are probably due to brain maturation, as well as to social learning. Patients with ASPD and BPD will no longer meet criteria if they are less impulsive after 5 or 10 years. This does not mean, however, that their interpersonal problems are behind them.

The findings of these follow-back studies needed to be supplemented by large-scale prospective follow-ups and needed to be generalized to a larger population suffering from a wider range of PDs. The National Institute of Mental Health made a major investment in sponsoring the Collaborative Longitudinal Study of Personality Disorders (CLPS), a 10-year prospective follow-up of patients with four diagnoses: borderline, schizotypal, avoidant, and obsessive–compulsive (Gunderson et al., 2011). In each category, symptoms remitted with time, and many patients eventually functioned within a normal range. These findings clearly showed that improvement over time is standard for PD. Even if some patients continue to have difficulties with work and interpersonal relations, the vast majority no longer met criteria when evaluated after 10 years.

Another important prospective study, the McLean Study of Adult Development, compares BPD patients with patients with other PDs, all of whom had been hospitalized (Zanarini, Frankenburg, Reich, & Fitzmaurice, 2012). This research has now lasted 20 years and seems ready to continue to evaluate patients into old age. The results have been essentially identical to those of the CLPS study in documenting that remission is the usual outcome and that once patients remit, they rarely relapse. However, although recovery was the rule, many patients had residual difficulties in psychosocial functioning. (This suggests that some patients may need additional treatment later in adult life.)

Similar findings emerged from the Longitudinal Study of Personality Disorders, which followed college students into adult life (Lenzenweger, 1999). There was good evidence for improvement over time, even for highly symptomatic disorders such as BPD.

In summary, patients with PDs have a reasonably good prognosis, and most do better than patients with mood disorders. It would be useful if clinicians knew more about these findings, because they might be less pessimistic and less reluctant to make PD diagnoses. Although none of the studies was able to test whether treatment makes a difference, it seems reasonable to consider that therapy aims to speed up the process of recovery and to make it more complete.

I now make a point of explaining the BPD diagnosis to all patients and informing them that while their condition is serious, they can be expected to recover. This hopeful message is supported by the scientific evidence, and many patients are glad to hear it. One told me, "I thought I was just this weird person who didn't respond to antidepressants, but now I know I have a completely different problem."

TWO

SPECIFIC DISORDERS

5

Antisocial Personality Disorder

For as long as he could remember, Johnnie had always been in trouble. He was a defiant and aggressive child, and his parents could not control him. He had been tossed out of several schools, and only finished Grade 9. Johnnie began smoking pot before puberty and then moved on to heavy use of alcohol and cocaine. By age 16, he was a drug dealer. Johnnie was often brought to the attention of the police for incidents ranging from theft to violent quarrels when intoxicated. His first sexual experiences were at age 12, and he went on to have many brief affairs without making a commitment to anyone. Although peripherally involved with organized crime, he was never loyal to anyone.

At 25, Johnnie, who was unemployed, was charged with assault after a drunken encounter with a policeman. In the past, his parents had always bailed him out of trouble, but this was a second offense, so this time they hired a good lawyer. He came to the psychiatric clinic asking for support

http://dx.doi.org/10.1037/14642-006
A Concise Guide to Personality Disorders, by J. Paris

for a defense of mental illness. He even asked if the clinic could do a brain scan, which could show that he was not responsible for his behavioral problems.

Johnnie is a typical example of antisocial personality disorder (ASPD), a condition that is common but more often seen in forensic settings.

HISTORY

Two hundred years ago, the only generally recognized mental illnesses were psychoses and severe depressions that required hospitalization (Shorter, 1997). There was not yet any concept of personality disorder (PD). From time to time, however, nonpsychotic patients would be referred to mental hospitals after committing serious crimes if these crimes involved violent or bizarre actions without an obvious motive. The term *moral insanity* was used to describe such cases (Berrios, 1993).

In the 20th century, a number of different (and often confusing) terms have been used to describe offenders who are callous or chronically criminal in their behavior. *Sociopathy* and *psychopathy* have been used for at least a hundred years, but they are not interchangeable (Rutter, 2006).

The first edition of the *Diagnostic and Statistical Manual of Mental Disorders* (*DSM–I;* American Psychiatric Association, 1952) included a category of *sociopathic personality*, which the second edition (*DSM–II;* American Psychiatric Association, 1968) went on to rename ASPD. To make things more complicated, the *International Classification of Diseases* (World Health Organization, 1993) chose the term *dissocial.* Yet although *antisocial personality*, *dissocial personality*, and *sociopathy* all describe more or less the same construct, *psychopathy* is different.

Hervey Cleckley (1964) wrote a classic book on psychopathy, which, in a clever turn of phrase, he titled *The Mask of Sanity.* For Cleckley, psychopaths were mentally ill, even if that wasn't immediately obvious. These were patients who, in addition to a criminal history, were charming, manipulative, and (most particularly) callous about other people's feelings. Cleckley thought psychopaths were born that way, and he included many dramatic tales of bad children coming from good families. However, his experience was that of a private practitioner attending to children of the wealthy; a forensic specialist would have observed a different pattern, in which dysfunctional families produce dysfunctional children. This is what Lee Robins (1966) found in a landmark prospective study.

The Canadian psychologist Robert Hare (1999) has carried out a lifetime of research on psychopathy in forensic populations. His Psychopathy Checklist (PCL–R; Hare, 2003) is a structured interview used in hundreds of research studies. Hare (2003) has shown that scores on the PCL–R require a two-factor model: one mainly describing criminal behavior, the other describing personality traits of callousness and manipulativeness. In contrast, ASPD describes a wider range of people with less severe behavioral patterns (Coid, 2009).

CHARACTERISTICS

The criteria for ASPD in *DSM–5* (American Psychiatric Association, 2013) are based on a disregard for the rights of others (callousness, criminality, impulsivity, irresponsibility) and on a past history of conduct disorder (CD). Unlike other PDs, this diagnosis can only be made after age 18 years. The reason is that CD sometimes "burns out" by the end of adolescence. However, it is possible in *DSM–5* to score severe callousness as a *specifier*. This procedure could help researchers identify patients who meet the more stringent requirements for psychopathy.

The construct of ASPD derives from the work of a sociologist (Robins, 1966) who followed up a large cohort of children with CD into adulthood. The main finding was that if children did not have CD, they would not develop ASPD as adults. However, not all children with CD became antisocial. That outcome is more likely in the presence of an earlier onset and greater severity (Zoccolillo, Pickles, Quinton, & Rutter, 1992). Also, when CD starts in adolescence, the clinical picture is more sensitive to social context, is associated with gang membership, and often remits by young adulthood (Moffitt, 1993).

ASPD can be mistaken for other diagnoses. For example, if these patients are arrested or put in jail, they may threaten or attempt suicide, but that need not be a picture of clinical depression. Another mistake is that ASPD, when it presents in an emergency department, can be misdiagnosed as mania. Taking a careful life history and obtaining additional information from family members helps avoid these errors.

PREVALENCE

ASPD is a highly prevalent disorder. Moran (1999) described its frequency as between 2% and 3%, and the National Epidemiologic Survey on Alcohol and Related Conditions estimated prevalence at 3.7%. In all studies, the diagnosis is much more common in males than females. Among prisoners, approximately half will meet criteria (Black, Gunter, Loveless, Allen, & Sieleni, 2010; Fazel & Danesh, 2002; Moran, 1999).

However, ASPD appears to be rare in non-Western countries in which a more traditional way of life has been maintained. The prevalence is also low in Western countries that have retained stronger traditions. Thus, in a Norwegian survey, the prevalence was only 0.7% (Torgersen, Kringlen, & Cramer, 2001). In a study in Taiwan conducted approximately 30 years ago (Hwu, Yeh, & Chang, 1989), almost no cases could be found, either in urban or in rural samples. The results might be different today because Taiwan has become more like Europe and North America.

RISK FACTORS

The risk factors for ASPD are biological, psychological, and social. Biological factors definitely increase the risk for developing ASPD. Criminality, impulsivity, and callousness, the key characteristics of the disorder, are, like other personality traits, clearly heritable (Mednick, Moffitt, & Stack, 2009). Some of these traits can identified early in development; in one longitudinal study, observations of aggressiveness during a 90-minute interview at age 3 predicted antisocial behavior at age 18 (Caspi, Moffitt, Newman, & Silva, 1996).

No biomarkers are known to correlate with antisocial traits, but Adrian Raine (2013), a researcher at the University of Pennsylvania, conducted a series of studies that point to brain differences in violent criminals. His group used imaging to identify abnormalities in frontal white matter, as well as more subtle anatomical changes. The research suggests a problem with brain connectivity, affecting regions associated with the processing of emotion and the control of impulsivity. However, most patients with ASPD are not consistently violent, and many have never been in prison (Robins, 1966). Therefore, these results cannot be generalized to all individuals who meet diagnostic criteria.

Gene–environment interactions are important in the risk for ASPD. An adoption study by Cloninger, Sigvardsson, Bohman, and van Knorring (1982) found that interactions between temperament and family adversity accounted for the risk for ASPD risk better than either alone. In one of the most widely quoted studies in the history of psychology, Caspi et al. (2002) found that a combination of heritable risk (the gene controlling monoamine oxidase) and child abuse predicted antisocial behavior, yet neither of these risk factors did so by themselves. This finding remains controversial because it has not always been replicated, and it is worth noting that only a subgroup in this cohort developed antisocial characteristics.

Family dysfunction is a strong risk factor for ASPD (Black, 2013a). Many patients grow up in families characterized by chaos and violence, and physical abuse is common (J. Hill, 2003). Others suffer from a lack of the structure and discipline they need to control their impulsivity (Robins, 1966). A chaotic family environment may also reflect common heritable vulnerabilities in both parents and children. Unfortunately, the literature on psychosocial adversity is not extensive, reflecting the fact that patients with ASPD do not often come for treatment in mental health settings, and when they do, they are difficult to recruit for research.

Social factors play an important role in ASPD. Callousness and criminality have always characterized certain people, as history clearly shows, but, as noted in Chapter 3, there was a notable increase in the prevalence of ASPD after the Second World War (Rutter & Smith, 1995), suggesting that rapid social change can make these problems more prevalent. This hypothesis is also supported by cross-cultural differences in the prevalence of the disorder (Hwu et al., 1989).

In summary, only the most severe cases of ASPD point to a "bad seed" theory. In those patients, callousness seems to represent a defect, either in the capacity for empathy or in the emotional consequences that accompany empathy. This is why some patients do well in combat situations during times of war but fail to adapt to the expectations of a peacetime life. For less severe cases, heritable biological risks may account for a smaller portion of the variance. Many patients grow up in dysfunctional families and are raised in bad neighborhoods and associate with problematic peer groups that do not provide them with positive role models. Thus, interactions among biological, psychological, and social risk factors are required to explain the pathways to this form of psychopathology.

OUTCOME

The outcome of ASPD is similar to those of other impulsive disorders, such as substance abuse or borderline PD. In a unique study, Black, Baumgard, and Bell (1995) followed 71 patients for several decades who had found their way, at least briefly, into a mental hospital. Thirty years later, they continued to have serious problems holding a job and maintaining intimate relations. Yet these former patients no longer showed the behavioral patterns that had led them to be in repeated trouble with the legal system. Thus, ASPD shows some of the features of burnout seen in impulsive disorders such as substance abuse. For this reason, it is generally (but not always) safe to release middle-aged patients from prison. Even so, the prognosis of ASPD remains guarded. Black et al. (1995) observed that these patients, even when they no longer met diagnostic criteria, continued to be difficult people.

MANAGING ASPD

Unless you work in a forensic setting or a substance abuse clinic, you may not often see patients with ASPD. Help seeking is not the forte of this population. However, cases of ASPD do sometimes appear for assessment in clinics. Zimmerman, Rothschild, and Chelminski (2005) found that 3.6% of outpatients meet diagnostic criteria for the disorder. A common scenario is for them to come on the advice of lawyers who hope to get them off a charge.

There has been concern about the potential for violence among patients with this diagnosis. In prisons, up to half of the population will meet criteria for ASPD (Black, Gunter, Loveless, Allen, & Sieleni, 2010). In response to some notorious crimes, the National Health Service in the United Kingdom set up units for "dangerous and severe personality disorder" (Mullen, 2007). However, most people with the diagnosis never kill anyone.

By and large, patients with ASPD do not benefit from talking therapies. The only study, never replicated, suggesting that standard methods might help them was conducted 30 years ago by Woody, McLellan, Luborsky, and O'Brien (1985), but the sample was small, the patients were already in treatment for substance abuse, and they were all clinically depressed. Because patients with ASPD have a high rate of substance abuse (Grant et al., 2004), drug rehabilitation (Fridell, Hesse, Jaeger, & Kühlhorn, 2008) may be the useful intervention. Successful withdrawal from addictive drugs may improve functioning even when patients continue to show features of their PD.

Another twist in the story is that some of the women therapists treat are attracted to antisocial men, like the proverbial moth to the flame. These men may be callous, but they can be surprisingly good at using empathy to manipulate women (as well as other people in their lives). Many of these couples end up in situations of domestic violence.

There is no reason at this point to doubt the overall conclusion that patients with ASPD are not suitable for psychotherapy, at least in the standard forms by which it is currently applied. Thus, one reason why making the diagnosis is important is that recognizing ASPD allows therapists to save their limited time for more treatable cases. If we did have a treatment for ASPD, whether biological or psychological, the demand would be enormous, given the high social cost of the disorder. At this point, however, therapy for substance abuse may be the most reasonable option we have to offer.

6

Borderline Personality Disorder

Laura was a 29-year-old woman with a long psychiatric history who came to the emergency department with suicidal ideas. She had been seen as an adolescent for recurrent overdoses, cutting, and substance use, but she had not engaged in therapy. Laura finished high school and then supported herself for some time working as a stripper before taking a job in customer service. She described her unstable mood as a roller-coaster. Relationships with men began quickly and ended badly. Many of her boyfriends were abusive, and at least two were active criminals. Breakups were difficult and had often led to visits to the emergency department or to crisis clinics. When highly stressed, Laura felt depersonalized and paranoid and sometimes heard voices telling her to kill herself. She thought of suicide every day but still hoped that she could be treated for her problems.

This vignette describes a typical case of borderline personality disorder (BPD), the most important personality disorder (PD) in clinical

http://dx.doi.org/10.1037/14642-007
A Concise Guide to Personality Disorders, by J. Paris

practice and one of the most extensively researched. BPD is common and can be identified in approximately 10% of patients in mental health clinics (Zimmerman, Rothschild, & Chelminski, 2005). That is why it plays such a prominent role in this book.

CLINICAL FEATURES

Adolf Stern (1938), the psychoanalyst who first described BPD, thought that this kind of psychopathology lay on some kind of border between neurosis and psychosis. Despite this misleading theory, and a confusing choice of a name, Stern's description of what BPD patients are like remains contemporary. The term *borderline* is a misnomer and has only been retained for lack of a good alternative, much as *schizophrenia* does not really describe a split mind. Although alternative names have been suggested, terms such as *emotional dysregulation disorder* capture only one element of the clinical picture. We should not change the name until the condition is much better understood.

BPD has a closer resemblance to severe mental disorders than to other PDs. It has an unusually wide range of comorbidity and is associated with intense suffering and a wide range of symptoms, including dysregulation of mood and anxiety, substance abuse, and micropsychotic symptoms (Gunderson & Links, 2012; Paris, 2007c; Zanarini, Frankenburg, Khera, & Bleichmar, 2001). Because patients with this diagnosis suffer, they are highly treatment seeking (Zanarini et al., 2001).

BPD is an amalgam of traits and symptoms. A large body of research shows that the most prominent of its underlying traits are affective instability and impulsivity (Crowell, Beauchaine, & Linehan, 2009; Siever & Davis, 1991). Thus, many of its clinical features can be understood as reflecting emotion dysregulation, combined with a wide range of impulsive actions, both of which lead to serious and chronic interpersonal problems. These underlying traits of BPD are only partially egosyntonic. Patients complain about unstable mood, described as a "roller-coaster" of emotions in response to environmental stressors, and most acknowledge that impulsive actions get them into difficulty (Linehan, 1993; Paris, 2008a). Although impulsive actions, such as substance abuse, sexual promiscuity, and shop-lifting, can be egosyntonic, this is not the case for self-harm behaviors such as cutting or for overdoses. Finally, the cognitive symptoms of BPD, such as depersonalization, paranoid ideas, and transitory auditory hallucinations (Zanarini, Frankenburg, Wedig, & Fitzmaurice, 2013; Zanarini, Gunderson, & Frankenburg, 1990), are almost always egodystonic.

None of these dimensions account for the most severe symptoms asso-ciated with BPD, such as chronic suicidality and self-harm, but as patients recover, those symptoms tend to remit. Even after recovery, patients often retain "subsyndromal" features related to dysfunctional traits that do not change, most particularly mood instability that interferes with occupation and interpersonal functioning (Zanarini et al., 2007).

Recurrent overdoses, a feature seen in most patients with BPD (Soloff, Lynch, Kelly, Malone, & Mann, 2000), contrasts with a frequency of only 5% for lifetime suicide attempts in the general population (Kessler, Berglund, Borges, Nock, & Wang, 2005). Patients with BPD can also have suicidal ide-ation for years on end, a phenomenon that, when present, strongly suggests the diagnosis (Paris, 2008a). Although adolescents experiment with cutting, the pattern is usually transient and remits over the course of development (Moran et al., 2012). In contrast, BPD patients persist with self-harm for years, and because this behavior has modulating effects on dysphoria, can become addicted to cutting (Brown, Comtois, & Linehan, 2002). These phenomena are only partially explained by high levels of neuroticism (Morey et al., 2007; Morey & Zanarini, 2000), which describe emotion dys-regulation without specifying behaviors that could be used for emotion regulation. Finally, approximately 10% of BPD patients eventually commit suicide (Paris, 2008a).

Because BPD is associated with such a broad range of symptoms, the disorder can seem complex and mystifying. Given the range of its clinical features, BPD might be called psychiatry's chameleon. It does not easily fit into a single diagnostic niche, and because symptoms are so widespread, it overlaps with many other diagnoses. The meaning of these comorbidities has sometimes been interpreted as meaning that BPD is "really" something other than a PD. Perhaps all they show, however, is that the *Diagnostic and*

Statistical Manual of Mental Disorders (*DSM*) system uses similar criteria to describe many disorders. Because severe PDs disrupt psychosocial functioning, it should be no surprise that patients are depressed, anxious, and moody.

The idea that BPD is a variant of some other disorder has been influential among clinicians who find the construct confusing and treatment options murky. It has long been proposed that BPD is a form of depression (Akiskal et al., 1985), a variant of bipolarity (Akiskal, 2004), or a "complex" form of posttraumatic stress disorder (PTSD; Herman, 1992). Each of these theories is like the blind men and the elephant—they consider only one domain of the disorder, not BPD as a whole. The disorder is complex, but this diagnosis allows us to use a single construct to describe mood symptoms, anxiety symptoms, substance abuse, cognitive symptoms, and problematic relationships.

In this way, a diagnosis of BPD covers more ground. As is so often the case, a PD construct explains more than a number of accompanying "comorbidities." The mood symptoms of BPD are intrinsic to the diagnosis but reflect affective instability rather than classical mood disorder (Gunderson & Links, 2012). Depressed mood in BPD also does not respond to standard treatments, such as pharmacotherapy (Stoffers, Völlm, et al., 2012), indicating that it is an entirely different phenomenon.

Two comorbid diagnoses are particularly important when one is considering how to treat BPD. The first is substance abuse: Although most patients with BPD use substances on a casual basis, some have serious addictions. The second is eating disorders: Severe bulimia or anorexia nervosa can take over patients' lives. When substance abuse and eating disorders are severe, they have to be treated first, before the PD can be usefully addressed (Gunderson & Links, 2012).

Practitioners who do not recognize BPD (because all they see is a mood disorder) will apply clinical tools that are not ideal for PDs. Psychiatrists may prefer pharmacological interventions, while clinical psychologists may apply their training in cognitive–behavioral methods to manage anxiety or depression. Often it is only when these treatments fail that consultation with a specialist in PD occurs.

Yet experienced consultants can usually (but not always) make a diagnosis of BPD in a single interview. What one has to do is move beyond current symptoms and obtain a detailed life history. There can be heterogeneity, but for me, patients who meet most of the diagnostic criteria seem like peas in a pod. The key point is that knowing how to recognize this disorder allows you to make a choice of therapy guided by diagnosis.

THE MULTIPLE DOMAINS OF BPD

BPD describes multiple domains of psychopathology (Paris, 2007c). Many clinicians have been impressed by its prominent mood symptoms. These patients have strong emotional responses to life circumstances and take a long time to calm down. However, they are not always chronically depressed, and intense anger is a feature of the disorder. Moreover, instead of episodes of depression or hypomania, in which affect is stable and unresponsive to the environment, emotions have a mercurial quality. Unlike depression (defined in the fifth edition of the *DSM* [*DSM–5*] as lasting for at least 2 weeks) or hypomania (defined in *DSM–5* as lasting for at least 4 days), patients with BPD can be in a different mood from hour to hour, depending on what is going on in their interpersonal life.

Thus, one of the most characteristic features of the disorder is *affective instability* (AI; Koenigsberg, 2010), which is essentially identical to *emotion dysregulation* (ED; Linehan, 1993). AI and ED result from hypersensitivity to the environment and show rapid and intense responses, followed by a slow recovery, and occur when interpersonal interactions are conflictual (Russell, Moskowitz, Zuroff, Sookman, & Paris, 2007). Again, note that AI is different from clinical depression (during which nothing can cheer up the patient) or hypomanic episodes (during which patients remain "high" even when things go wrong). Also, unlike patients with mood disorders, BPD patients are prone to becoming angry, often to the point of screaming, breaking things, or even becoming physically violent.

Affective instability in BPD patients, unlike classical mood disorders, responds inconsistently, or not at all, to pharmacotherapy, including antidepressants, mood stabilizers, and antipsychotics (Stoffers, Völlm, et al.,

2012). Finally, mood in BPD is associated with feelings of emptiness and chronic suicidality (Gunderson & Links, 2012).

BPD should be easy to diagnose, but because of its prominent mood features, it is often mistaken for bipolar disorder. These days almost every patient with BPD will be called bipolar by someone, particularly when they come to an emergency department. Moreover, there is a group of zealots for bipolarity who describe the mood shifts of BPD as lying within a "bipolar spectrum" (Akiskal, 2004). This point of view leads to the treatment of BPD with multiple medications that do not work, as opposed to the use of specialized psychotherapies that do work.

There are a number of reasons to reject the conclusion that BPD is a form of bipolarity (Paris, Gunderson, & Weinberg, 2007). BPD and bipolar disorders can co-occur, but their relationship is neither consistent nor specific. There are important differences in phenomenology. They do not show the same response to medication. Family studies point to clear distinctions, and it is unusual for BPD to evolve into bipolar disorder. Finally, research has not shown that these disorders have a common etiology.

The second core feature of BPD is impulsivity. Moeller, Barratt, Dougherty, Schmitz, and Swann (2001) defined this construct as describing (a) decreased sensitivity to *negative* consequences of behavior; (b) rapid, unplanned reactions to stimuli before complete processing of information; and (c) lack of regard for long-term consequences. Although other mental disorders also show impulsivity, there are a number of characteristic impulsive behaviors seen in BPD. These consist of chronic and recurrent overdoses and self-harm behaviors such as cutting. These are the symptoms that often bring BPD patients to the emergency department, where BPD can be found in approximately 40% of patients presenting with repetitive suicide attempts (Forman, Berk, Henriques, Brown, & Beck, 2004). One also sees a wide range of other impulsive actions, most particularly substance abuse, bulimia, and shoplifting (Zanarini et al., 2001).

BPD can be frightening because patients with this diagnosis frequently have chronic suicidality—threatening to kill themselves or making multiple attempts. This is why some therapists avoid treating them. Yet although suicidality in BPD is a primary object of clinical concern, it is chronic. Some patients will think about killing themselves on a daily basis for years, and up to 10% of patients with BPD eventually do commit suicide; some come close after making serious attempts (Paris, 2008a). This outcome is more likely in patients who are unusually impulsive or aggressive (McGirr, Paris, Lesage, Renaud, & Turecki, 2007). Those who kill themselves are usually older (approximately 35–40 years of age) and have failed to recover from the disorder even in the face of multiple attempts at treatment (Paris, 2003).

Despite the long-term risk, 90% of patients with BPD never kill themselves (Paris, 2006). This is crucial for frightened clinicians to keep in mind. For the most part, suicidality in BPD is communicative—a way of turning up the volume when one does not expect to be heard. Paradoxically, maintaining the option of suicide can also be comforting, particularly when quality of life is low. Nonetheless, overdoses are common in BPD. Fortunately, most incidents involve taking pills impulsively and at nonlethal levels, but some patients raise the stakes higher, and a scenario can develop that looks like a version of Russian roulette, with the stakes being life and death.

It is also important to know that self-harm, particularly cutting, is not suicidal behavior. BPD patients may cut their wrists and arms (or their thighs and abdomen if they want to avoid having other people notice). The purpose, as reported by patients themselves (Brown, Comtois, & Linehan, 2002), is to relieve tension, not to die. Self-harm is used to break the vicious cycles associated with emotional dysregulation. Its effectiveness in managing painful affects explains why these behaviors, however problematic, can sometimes become addictive (Linehan, 1993).

In addition to affective instability and impulsivity, patients with BPD have highly unstable intimate relationships. Their closest attachments, usually to romantic partners, are characterized by clinging, fear of abandonment, and intense conflict (Gunderson & Links, 2012). Gunderson and Lyons-Ruth (2008) suggested primacy be given to the interpersonal aspects of the disorder. However, these features are also a consequence of emotion dysregulation. If what patients need from an intimate partner is a soothing response, and they don't get it, they may respond with anger, leading to further escalation of the conflict.

The most "borderline" aspect of BPD is its cognitive symptoms (Zanarini et al., 2013). About half of all patients experience transitory auditory hallucinations under stress, but they do not develop delusional elaborations of such experiences. One of the most common symptoms is hearing a voice saying the patient is bad and should die. Sometimes the experience seems temporarily real, but on reflection, patients realize that they are hearing their own thoughts spoken aloud.

Many BPD patients experience paranoid feelings: They are suspicious and think others, even strangers, are talking about them, but these features do not reach delusional proportions. Finally, depersonalization and derealization in BPD can be severe and prolonged. These symptoms are sometimes termed *dissociative*, but it is not clear that is a helpful term. By and large, they are not related to specific life experiences but reflect emptiness and interpersonal disconnection.

The clinical features of BPD are listed in *DSM–5* (American Psychiatric Association, 2013), with five of nine required to make a diagnosis (i.e., a *polythetic* system). No single feature is necessary, and *DSM*'s approach has sometimes been called a "Chinese menu." The problem is that there are too many ways for patients with different symptoms to meet criteria for the same diagnosis. For that reason, some researchers prefer a more restrictive definition, grouping symptoms into symptomatic or trait dimensions and requiring more characteristic features to be present.

I have had long experience in using a semistructured interview developed at McLean Hospital in Boston, based on criteria developed 40 years ago by Gunderson and Singer (1975). The Diagnostic Interview for Borderlines, Revised (DIB–R; Zanarini, Gunderson, Frankenburg, & Chauncey, 1989) describes a more homogeneous group of patients than *DSM–5*. Symptoms are scored on four subscales (affective, cognitive, impulsive, and interpersonal), and diagnosis requires having most of them, with the last two subscales (impulsive and interpersonal), reflecting the core aspects of the disorder, being more heavily weighted. Patients cannot reach the cutoff point (a score of 8 of 10) without having multiple features of the disorder, and thus heterogeneity is greatly reduced.

Some patients who meet *DSM* criteria will not meet DIB–R criteria, either because they never had or no longer have a group of symptoms. For example, patients who have partially recovered from BPD but have come to avoid intimate relationships will not score on the DIB–R, which requires a score of 8 of 10 for problems present over the past 2 years. One can modify this requirement to describe a group of "lifetime" borderline patients who no longer meet criteria and have "graduated" to a diagnosis of PD—not otherwise specified. As we will see, this kind of partial recovery is one of the most common outcomes for patients with BPD.

Because research on the characteristic features of BPD seems clear-cut, why is it so often missed? To make a diagnosis, one must differentiate a PD from symptomatic conditions that resemble it or that may sometimes accompany it. The first of such conditions is major depression. There is little doubt that patients with BPD often present with symptoms that meet *DSM–5* criteria for major depression. This leads to the common practice of diagnosing a depression but either ignoring the PD, or, under previous editions of *DSM*, writing a comment such as "Axis II, deferred." However, consider the low bar that *DSM–5* makes for a diagnosis of "major depression." It only requires the presence of five of nine symptoms for a period as brief as 2 weeks. This leads to confusion between sadness or unhappiness and depressive illness (A. V. Horwitz & Wakefield, 2007). In BPD, patients can be depressed and then shift rapidly into another mood (Gunderson & Phillips, 1991). Even when they do cross the 2-week bar for a major depression, they do not respond to the same treatment as patients who have depression without a PD (Newton-Howes, Tyrer, & Johnson, 2006). Finally, depression in BPD is not an episode but a chronic state that is similar to a feeling of emptiness (Gunderson & Phillips, 1991).

A second confounding condition is bipolar disorder. As discussed earlier, because mood swings in BPD are rapid and mercurial, they do not meet the 4-day requirement for hypomania, which is, in turn, a requirement for a diagnosis of bipolar II disorder. However, for those who remain convinced that the PD is a bipolar variant, *DSM–5* allows them to make a diagnosis of *bipolar disorder, unspecified* or *bipolar disorder, other specified*. The manual allows this category to be applied to patients who have the typical affective instability associated with BPD. (It can also be used for atypical presentations such as bipolar II without depression.) Although one rarely sees this diagnosis in practice (no one really wants to use these residual categories), the very presence of this option reflects a belief in the validity of a bipolar spectrum.

The third is attention-deficit/hyperactivity disorder (ADHD). This diagnosis has become extremely common in adults and is considered by Batstra and Frances (2012) to be a fad producing an "epidemic." ADHD has become a frequent diagnosis in adults largely because it is the basis for drug prescriptions or specific interventions by psychologists (Paris, 2013d). However, not all attention problems in adults justify a diagnosis of ADHD. For one thing, you cannot make the diagnosis without documenting a childhood onset, which many clinicians fail to do. Moreover, PDs such as BPD can be associated with an unfocused style of life in which goals are not set or reached, combined with a pattern of impulsivity. This picture can be confused with the specific deficits of ADHD, but because there is no evidence that stimulants have any value in BPD, this is likely to be an error.

EPIDEMIOLOGY

Most studies of the community prevalence of BPD find a rate somewhat less than 1% (Coid, Yang, Tyrer, Roberts, & Ullrich, 2006; Lenzenweger, Lane, Loranger, & Kessler, 2007; Torgersen, Kringlen, & Cramer, 2001), about the same as for schizophrenia. As already noted, higher frequencies are probably an artifact of conducting large-scale surveys with research assistants as interviewers.

Studies have been conducted in which men with BPD were examined separately, with few clinical differences from women (Paris, Zweig-Frank, & Guzder, 1994b). Although most BPD patients in clinical settings are female, community studies have found an equal prevalence in men and women (Lenzenweger et al., 2007). The question is how to account for this difference. The most likely explanation is that women are more likely to seek help. Notably, patients with BPD who die by suicide are usually male, and most have only intermittent contact with the mental health system (Lesage et al., 1994). Men with the same level of psychopathology are more likely to live in the world of substance abuse.

A BIOPSYCHOSOCIAL MODEL OF BPD

The biopsychosocial model (Engel, 1980) proposes that the etiology of mental disorders is based on complex interactions among biological vulnerability, psychological adversity, and social stressors. BPD is a good example of its usefulness.

Biological Factors

The heritability of BPD accounts for more than half of the variance (Reichborn-Kjennerud et al., 2013). Yet how do genes affect brain function to make people vulnerable to the disorder? We do not know the answer. There is no such thing as a gene "for" BPD, and many variations probably play a role.

What we do know is that the brain functions differently in patients with BPD (New, Goodman, Triebwasser, & Siever, 2008). This is a large and complex literature, but the most consistent findings are related to the traits of affective instability and impulsivity that underlie the diagnosis. Neuroimaging findings have been well summarized by New, Goodman, Triebwasser, and Siever (2008). As discussed in Chapter 3 of this volume, there is a diminished top-down control of affective responses related to deceased responsiveness of specific regions of prefrontal cortex, as well as functional and volumetric changes in subcortical structures such as amygdala, hippocampus, and caudate. Neuroendocrine research also points to a role for serotonin in the impulsivity that characterizes BPD.

Evidently, BPD patients are wired differently. However, there is no predictable relationship between abnormalities in connectivity or neurotransmission and the disorder. Without psychosocial adversity, temperamental characteristics remain temperamental. Patients who have recovered from BPD may continue to be highly emotional, but they learn with time to contain intense feelings and not act on them in ways that are self-destructive (Paris, 2003).

Psychological Factors

The psychosocial adversities that convert temperamental vulnerability to a diagnosable PD have been widely documented, with most findings pointing to child abuse, emotional neglect, and dysfunctional families (Paris, 2008a; Zanarini, 2000). Again, there is no predictable relationship between these risks and the development of the disorder. As shown by our own research on sibling pairs that are discordant for BPD (Laporte, Paris, Guttman, & Russell, 2011), childhood adversity has a different effect on people with a vulnerable temperament than on those who have traits that promote resilience. Also, about a third of patients with BPD will not have experienced serious adversity in childhood (Paris, 2008a).

There is no simple relationship between trauma and BPD. This is why the concept of *complex PTSD* or *complex trauma* (Herman, 1992) is misleading. It supposes that disorders like BPD are a direct result of childhood experiences, which is not the case. Moreover, throwing around words such as *complex* is little more than hand-waving and explains nothing about the truly complex pathways that lead to BPD.

To understand BPD, one must take gene–environment interactions into account. For example, a recent study of BPD traits that used a twin sample to assess genetic influences failed to find a direct relationship between child abuse and BPD traits (Bornovalova, Huibregste, & Hicks, 2013).

To understand these mechanisms, one must consider that heritable traits of affective instability make children more sensitive to their environment, which can then lead to vicious cycles in which negative events further feed instability. Also, traits of impulsivity make children more likely to choose behaviors that reduce emotion dysregulation in the short run but increase it in the long run. Moreover, traumatic events are processed differently in those who are temperamentally vulnerable, but similar adversities produce either minor or no sequelae in most children (Fergusson & Mullen, 1999; Paris, 2000).

Our research group conducted a family study (Laporte et al., 2011) in a sample of severely ill women with BPD and their female siblings. Of 56 pairs of sisters, only three were concordant for the disorder. Yet both reported having been exposed to the same traumatic events. The sister who did develop BPD was distinguished by a different personality trait profile, pointing to the role of a problematic temperament.

In an earlier set of studies (Paris, Zweig-Frank, & Guzder, 1994a, 1994b), we found that approximately a third of BPD patients report severe abuse and neglect, a third had milder forms of adversity, and another third had a relatively normal childhood. These findings support a model in which developing BPD reflects what researchers refer to as a *common final pathway*, or what Cicchetti and Rogosch (2002) termed *equifinality*. Just as the same outcome can arise from different sources, different outcomes can arise from the same risk factors (i.e., *multifinality*).

Although many patients with BPD have a traumatic childhood, others will have suffered from having their intense emotions misunderstood. This is why Linehan (1993) hypothesized that BPD arises from interactions between temperamentally based emotion dysregulation with *invalidation* (the failure of family members to understand and support children when they are upset). Most research (Paris et al., 1994a, 1994b; Zanarini, 2000) suggests that in patients who have not had a traumatic childhood, feelings of emotional neglect are more important.

Thus, BPD patients can come to the same point after different experiences. Some come from highly dysfunctional families, and when we obtain such histories, we are tempted to say, "of course, this is why they have BPD." However, research showing the ubiquity of resilience suggests otherwise. When BPD patients come from relatively normal families in which their siblings do not have significant psychopathology, invalidation of emotions is a more likely mechanism. Yet for many years, some clinicians assumed that patients with BPD *must* have suffered child abuse; when patients did not actually remember such events, it was claimed that they had repressed these memories (Herman, 1992). There was a time in the late 1980s and into the 1990s when an epidemic of false memories of abuse, encouraged by therapists who believed in such theories, spread through the psychotherapy community (McNally, 2003). This was one of the most malignant fads in the history of psychiatry and clinical psychology. Although the tide of error has receded, there are still therapists who believe in these premises.

Social Factors

There is indirect evidence, based on increases in associated symptoms (e.g., suicidality, substance abuse), that BPD is more likely to develop when the social environment is stressful or changes too rapidly (Paris &

Lis, 2013). This mechanism could explain why BPD is a relatively recent diagnosis in psychiatry. It is also worth noting that some of the symptoms associated with the disorder are socially contagious, as in the current epidemic of self-harm in which some adolescents imitate these behaviors (Klonsky, 2007).

An Integrated Model

None of these risk factors produce a disorder by themselves, and all need to be placed in the frame of a biopsychosocial model. Only the effects of multiple and interacting risks can predict outcome, particularly one that can arise from several pathways (Beauchaine, Klein, Crowell, Derbidge, & Gatzke-Kopp, 2009).

Interactions between genes and environment are also consistent with a stress–diathesis model of mental disorders (Monroe & Simons, 1991). This leads to a general principle: Patients do not develop BPD unless they have an underlying temperamental vulnerability. In this respect, BPD resembles most severe mental disorders. There is an important role for environmental risks, but children who are resilient to childhood adversity probably have a different temperament from those who are not.

In summary, the recipe for cooking a case of BPD has many ingredients. This is why treatment requires multiple interventions that can also be biological, psychological, or social.

BPD OVER THE LIFE SPAN

Childhood Precursors and Adolescent Onset

BPD usually becomes clinically apparent during adolescence, and it may actually be more frequent at that stage than in young adult populations (Chanen & McCutcheon, 2013). Zanarini, Frankenburg, Khera, and Bleichmar (2001) found that most patients with BPD develop symptoms soon after puberty, even if they do not seek help until a few years later. Our own group (Biskin, Paris, Renaud, Raz, & Zelkowitz, 2011) followed a group of patients treated for BPD in mid-adolescence for 5 years and found that about half continued to meet criteria for the diagnosis in young adulthood. This is consistent with the course of BPD in young adulthood, in which some patients remit early but others take 10 to 15 years to recover (Gunderson et al., 2011).

Many clinicians are reluctant to diagnose PDs in teenagers because they may only be showing "adolescent turmoil" and may see problems as "just a phase." Actually, it is important to make the diagnosis in adolescent patients and not to dismiss these symptoms. It is also important not to attribute them to mood disorders without PD.

Although I often hear that *DSM* does not permit clinicians to make a valid PD diagnosis in adolescents, this idea is based on a mistaken reading of the manual. *DSM–5* allows for early diagnoses of any PD, with the exception of antisocial PD, but makes a point of requiring a chronic rather than an episodic course (at least a year of symptoms). Unfortunately, not everyone has read this passage carefully.

The onset of BPD at puberty is similar to the onset of mood disorders, psychoses, and addictions, all of which tend to present for the first time at that developmental landmark. Yet although the childhood precursors of ASPD are well known, we do not know what BPD patients were like as children. If we did, we might be in a position to consider strategies for prevention.

One possibility is that symptoms have been present before puberty but are more internalizing than externalizing, and thus they do not attract attention in the same way as conduct disorder. Some patients will describe feeling suicidal as children, although this is far from universal. Others state that life was manageable until puberty, when "all hell broke loose." Different developmental pathways can lead to a similar outcome.

In recent years, researchers have designed studies to examine the developmental precursors of BPD in children. Because women are more commonly seen in practice, the studies have focused on high-risk populations of girls. They have identified symptoms appearing before puberty that resemble BPD and that may suggest an early onset of the disorder (Stepp, Pilkonis, Hipwell, Loeber, & Stouthamer-Loeber, 2010; Zanarini et al., 2011). By age 11, some girls are affectively unstable, impulsive, and suicidal. The results of research thus far suggest that these girls have behavioral symptoms that can also be diagnosed as conduct disorder, oppositional defiant disorder, or ADHD and that they grow up in high-conflict dysfunctional families. Long-term follow-ups of these cohorts should shed light on whether women identified at this earlier stage are at risk for an adult diagnosis of BPD.

Long-Term Outcome

BPD, once believed to be a lifelong problem, turns out to have a better prognosis than severe mood disorders. Most patients stop meeting diagnostic criteria by middle age. This favorable outcome was first shown by retrospective (follow-back) studies (McGlashan, 1986; Paris, Brown, & Nowlis, 1987; Stone, 1990) and later confirmed by large-scale prospective studies (Gunderson et al., 2011; Zanarini, Frankenburg, Reich, & Fitzmaurice, 2012).

To summarize these findings, most patients with BPD do not meet criteria for the diagnosis at age 40, and many recover before age 30. Impulsive symptoms remit early, whereas affective symptoms are slower to change and are associated with some degree of interpersonal and cognitive problems. Some BPD patients recover completely, but many continue to have some degree of residual psychosocial dysfunction (Zanarini et al., 2012). Thus, even when patients are no longer acutely symptomatic, they may not find stable employment, stable partners, or become parents. In our 27-year follow-up (Paris & Zweig-Frank, 2001), although most BPD patients were working at age 50, only half were living with another person, and only half had ever had children.

Some of the most interesting and clinically relevant findings of outcome research concern suicide. The frequency of death by suicide in BPD is approximately 5% in prospectively followed cohorts and approximately 10% in follow-back studies (Paris, 2006). Although younger BPD patients frequently threaten to kill themselves, and frighten us by making such threats, the vast majority of suicides occur much later in the course of the illness. At least 90% of BPD patients, after being chronically suicidal for years, choose to go on living.

Our own research found that after 27 years of follow-up, the mean age of death by suicide was 38 (Paris & Zweig-Frank, 2001). Stone (1990) found a similar result: After 15 years, the mean age of suicide was 30. Thus, the highest risk of suicide in BPD does not lie in the early 20s, the period when patients are most likely to threaten suicide—and to alarm therapists. This was one of the most important research findings of my career. It confirms that in most patients with BPD, suicidal behaviors are largely interpersonal and communicative. The time when patients are most likely to kill themselves is after many treatments have been tried and have failed. By that point, while others have recovered from BPD, those most at risk have failed to improve.

TREATMENT

Unlike antisocial PD, BPD is treatable, and the main method of treatment is psychotherapy. Not any old psychotherapy will do, however. Standard methods do not work well. There are now a number of specific programs designed to meet the challenge of BPD. The most important of these is dialectical behavior therapy (DBT; Linehan, 1993). This is because DBT has the most evidence behind it and because most other methods apply rather similar principles. Anyone who wants to treat BPD has to understand this method and apply it to some extent.

However, despite the seminal contributions of DBT, it is lengthy, expensive, and not the only way to manage patients with BPD. This book argues for an integrative model that makes use of all the best ideas from all therapies currently available. It also argues for a briefer, more streamlined approach that makes therapy accessible for more patients. I discuss these recommendations in Chapter 10.

7

Narcissistic Personality Disorder

George was a 27-year-old man who had recently separated from his wife. She was an unusually attractive woman whom George considered a great catch; he was often gratified to see how other men envied him. However, their relationship floundered on his inability to meet her emotional needs or to compromise his lifestyle. Within a few years, he had become chronically unfaithful and had begun to use cocaine regularly. Although George had a good education, his performance at work could best be described as disappointing. Initially his employer was impressed with his creativity and offered him significant responsibility in the business, but George had a way of making big promises and not following through.

Although George was not clinically depressed, he sought therapy, which he saw as necessary for "self-realization." He also wanted to be treated by a therapist with a notable name and reputation.

http://dx.doi.org/10.1037/14642-008
A Concise Guide to Personality Disorders, by J. Paris

This vignette describes a typical case of narcissistic personality disorder (NPD), a condition that is common in clinical practice but that presents a challenge for standard methods of psychotherapy.

HISTORY

NPD is a controversial diagnosis. It has never been listed in the various editions of the *International Classification of Diseases.* It was included in the third edition of the *Diagnostic and Statistical Manual of Mental Disorders* (*DSM–III*; American Psychiatric Association, 1980), but as had been the case for borderline personality disorder (BPD), its close association with psychoanalysis limited its acceptance in the clinical community. Moreover, those who wrote about treating patients with NPD (Kernberg, 1976; Kohut, 1970) offered complex metapsychological speculations that were difficult to understand and not subject to empirical testing. More recently, however, NPD and narcissistic traits have been the subject of formal research (Campbell & Miller, 2011; Ogrodniczuk, 2013).

NPD had a rocky course in the development of the fifth edition of the *DSM* (*DSM–5*; American Psychiatric Association, 2013). Some said, jokingly, that this category had to be in the manual because narcissists can't stand being ignored, but the strength of the supporting data for the construct was questioned. At first, as the *DSM–5* proposals were being prepared, NPD was slated for elimination. Later, it was restored within the hybrid model, in which diagnosis depends on a characteristic trait profile. This definition can be found in Section III of *DSM–5.* However, in Section II of the manual, NPD was listed, along with other PDs, in the same way as in the fourth edition of the *DSM* (*DSM–IV*; American Psychiatric Association, 1994).

The future of the NPD diagnosis will depend on research. Studies have long been thin on the ground. Surveys also suggest that these patients do not present in large numbers in hospital centers (Zimmerman & Mattia, 1999). If they seek therapy at all, NPD patients will be found in private offices. Moreover, unlike BPD, NPD does not cause enough trouble to inspire clinicians to embark on systematic investigation.

Nonetheless, NPD is currently enjoying a revival, in part due to research by psychologists on narcissistic traits that are continuous with the disorder

(Campbell & Miller, 2011). The diagnosis describes difficulties that are almost purely egosyntonic, which helps explain why NPD is not common in hospital clinics.

Even so, research on narcissistic traits provides stronger support for the diagnosis than for some of the other categories that were never under threat of removal from *DSM–5*. Because traits are more continuous with NPD than is the case for either antisocial PD or BPD, what is found in people who have these traits will be applicable to those who meet criteria for a formal diagnosis.

CLINICAL FEATURES

NPD is described in *DSM–5* as characterized by an expectation to be recognized as superior and special (without superior accomplishments); a need for constant attention and admiration associated with envy; and with a preoccupation with success, attractiveness, power, and intelligence. NPD patients lack the ability to empathize with the feelings or desires of others, are arrogant, and expect special treatment. This seems like a witches' brew of egotism. Yet narcissistic patients can be initially attractive to other people, even if they always end up disappointing them.

As discussed in Chapter 2, NPD is an example of a disorder that is highly egosyntonic and that represents a pathological exaggeration of personality traits. Research supports the idea that narcissism and NPD lie on a continuum (Campbell & Miller, 2011). However, if patients do not recognize that their traits are problematic, that is just what makes NPD a clinical problem.

RISKS AND BENEFITS OF NARCISSISM

Narcissistic traits often lead to significant problems in work and relationships (Cain, Pincus, & Ansell, 2008). People with these characteristics overvalue themselves, are insufficiently self-critical, and respond to reasonable criticism with hurt and rage. When they suffer reversals in life, they are more likely to crash than to bounce back.

Even so, a small dose of narcissism can be adaptive in some contexts (Beck & Freeman, 2002). Being ambitious can be a good thing, and one cannot entirely fault people with unusual talents for being self-promoting, but people need to be willing to put in the effort required to make themselves a success, rather than expect rewards out of entitlement alone. We also need the interpersonal skills to work collaboratively with others.

Pathological narcissism differs from normal self-esteem. It is based on feelings of entitlement, as opposed to grounding one's sense of value in objective accomplishments (J. D. Miller, Gaughan, Pryor, Kamen, & Campbell, 2009). Narcissism is associated with manipulativeness and a lack of empathy, and this is why patients with NPD inevitably get into conflict with people who do not support their grandiosity. That is also why they lose jobs and intimate partners, even as they complain of being unappreciated.

PREVALENCE

Researchers have examined the prevalence of NPD in community and clinical populations. The National Epidemiologic Survey on Alcohol and Related Conditions study (Stinson et al., 2008) reported a surprisingly high prevalence (6.2%), yet once again the numbers seem inflated. The cutoff between traits and disorders requires clinical judgment, and ratings in this study were made by research assistants rather than by trained clinicians. A reanalysis of the same data applying a different cutoff for diagnosis (Trull, Jahng, Tomko, Wood, & Sher, 2010) yielded a much lower estimate: 0.7% for males and 1.2% for females. A systematic review of other published studies (Dhawan, Kunik, Oldham, & Coverdale, 2010) also found a mean community prevalence of 1%. The lower figure makes sense but still indicates that NPD is far from uncommon.

In clinical populations, NPD is seen somewhat more frequently. Some clinicians believe that these patients do not often present to clinics. Yet using systematic interviews, the largest study reported a prevalence of 2% (Zimmerman, Rothschild, & Chelminski, 2005). This suggests that despite the highly egosyntonic nature of NPD, patients with this diagnosis seek help when their lives go wrong. Research shows many patients with

NPD are distressed, lonely, and have poor social functioning (J. D. Miller & Campbell, 2010). They can become demoralized when their attempts to get others to meet their needs prove unsuccessful.

Fortunately, narcissism declines with age (Foster, Campbell, & Twenge, 2003). Most of us learn life's lessons and realize that we are not the center of the universe—or of anybody else's life, for that matter. For patients with a clinical diagnosis of NPD, that kind of learning may not take place. For this reason, they are more likely to be divorced and to become unemployed (Ronningstam, 2011).

Some researchers have suggested that not all NPD patients are overtly grandiose and that this disorder can also take a "covert-vulnerable" form (J. D. Miller, Hoffman, Campbell, & Pilkonis, 2008; J. D. Miller & Maples, 2012). That construct may have merit, but it expands the definition of NPD considerably. If grandiosity is not required, the diagnosis will have a much higher prevalence. (This could be one more example of how *DSM* diagnoses tend to expand with time.)

There has been some discussion in the literature as to whether narcissism is increasing in contemporary culture. Based on cohort changes in self-report data on the Narcissistic Personality Interview (NPI) from the 1960s to the 1980s compared with recent times, Twenge (2011) hypothesized a rapid increase in narcissism over recent decades. Twenge proposed that overindulgent parenting, a fad for-self-esteem, and a set of social expectations that apply to celebrities have created a culture that promotes narcissism. This idea has attracted attention, both in the professional community and in the popular media. One recent study (Park, Twenge, & Greenfield, 2014) found a recent decrease in narcissism scores associated with the economic recession that began in 2007.

However, in the absence of confirmation by prospective studies, the level of narcissism in the general population is difficult to measure. The jury is still out on this issue. My own view (Paris, 2013b), in accord with a concept developed by the American historian Christopher Lasch (1979), is that the decline of collectivism and the rise of individualism, which started to accelerate about a hundred years ago, was the beginning of our present "age of narcissism."

RISK FACTORS

Behavioral genetic studies of NPD (Torgersen et al., 2000), as well as of narcissistic traits (Vernon, Villani, Vickers, & Harris, 2008), have identified a heritable component that accounts for about 40% of total variance. This suggests that individuals are not likely to develop NPD without having a trait profile that makes them vulnerable. It is therefore logical that narcissistic traits, which can be observed in children (Twenge & Campbell, 2009), should precede the disorder. The existence of narcissism in prepubertal children has been documented by several research groups (P. L. Hill & Roberts, 2011; Kerig & Stellwagen, 2010; Tackett & Mackrell, 2011; Thomaes, Stegge, Bushman, Olthof, & Denissen, 2008). We need prospective follow-up of these cohorts into adulthood. Even if some children are prone to be boastful and grandiose (as many are), that would only be of concern if such characteristics do not mature in the course of development.

The psychological risk factors that amplify narcissistic traits to pathological narcissism have also been examined. Preliminary findings suggest a role for permissiveness in grandiose narcissism, and for cold overcontrol in vulnerable narcissism (Horton, 2011; Horton, Bleau, & Drwecki, 2006). These familial influences could also be augmented by cultural trends associated with the social reinforcement of grandiosity (Twenge & Campbell, 2009).

TREATMENT

There are surprisingly few data telling clinicians what works (and what doesn't work) for NPD. No clinical trials have ever been published. A large handbook of NPD and narcissism (Campbell & Miller, 2011) and an edited book on treatment (Ogrodniczuk, 2013) describe many potential methods of therapy, but none have yet been supported by clinical trials. In my view, we need a therapy package that is specific for NPD and that targets the most problematic areas of this disorder. This is what Linehan (1993) did for BPD, but NPD may require its own set of methods.

Psychoanalysts developed the NPD construct but usually relied on case histories with suspiciously happy endings. One might think that cognitive behavior therapy, which has a stronger research tradition, would have come up with some data, but no studies exist to support any of the ideas that have thus far been proposed.

These problems are all too common in the mental health field. The result is that we are forced to fall back on clinical experience. I can offer a little of my own, for what it is worth. In my younger days I treated quite a few patients with NPD. Like other people, I found them intriguing, at least initially. I saw them as people with potential who were wasting their talents. I was too inexperienced to see that mediocre abilities can be inflated by skills in self-promotion. At the time, I lived in an intellectual climate in which several of my colleagues were intensely interested in NPD, and several were commuting regularly to Chicago to get supervision from Heinz Kohut (the guru of NPD in the 1970s).

I gradually came to realize something every aspiring therapist should know. Patients with NPD like to talk and to be listened to attentively, but they are reluctant to change. Psychotherapy meets some of their needs but does not reduce their sense of entitlement. More generally, patients don't take therapy seriously unless they take ownership for their problems and suffer enough to feel psychic pain. These characteristics are deficient in NPD. Today, if I were asked which category of PD I would prefer to treat in therapy, it would almost certainly be BPD. These patients may be difficult, but they are unhappy with themselves, making them more motivated for treatment.

What might a program specifically designed for NPD look like? It would need to focus on the core traits and behavioral patterns that characterize this diagnosis. For example, patients would need to be taught why entitlement is a bad strategy and how to replace grandiosity with commitment, compassion, and a passion for making this a better world.

The problem with therapy for NPD is that people with this diagnosis may come for treatment because they are unhappy, but they are unlikely to recognize the nature of their problem. Narcissistic traits are highly ego-syntonic, and it may not even be possible to educate patients about their diagnosis. Moreover, treatment that is not well focused may do a better job at feeding emotional needs than at producing life changes. To counteract this tendency, we need to develop a model of individual therapy that is specifically designed to modify narcissistic traits. This is an ambitious goal, but no more so than in BPD, a condition long considered to be untreatable.

8

Other Personality Disorders

This book has devoted separate chapters to personality disorders (PDs) with a good research base. Most of the others have a smaller literature, so I discuss them more briefly here.

Schizotypal PD has a large empirical literature, mostly stimulated by a group led by Larry Siever of Mount Sinai Hospital in New York (Chemerinski, Triebwasser, Roussos, & Siever, 2013). However, schizotypal PD may not actually belong in the group of PDs; in the *International Classification of Diseases* (*ICD*) it is considered a mild form of schizophrenia (World Health Organization, 1993), whereas the fifth edition of the *Diagnostic and Statistical Manual of Mental Disorders* (*DSM–5*; American Psychiatric Association, 2013) lists it in both groupings.

The other PDs listed in *DSM–5* have attracted little research interest. Four (histrionic, schizoid, paranoid, and dependent) were removed in the proposals for *DSM–5* but restored to the classification when the hybrid

http://dx.doi.org/10.1037/14642-009
A Concise Guide to Personality Disorders, by J. Paris

proposal was rejected. The retention of two other categories (avoidant and obsessive–compulsive) may have been based on their having been examined for long-term outcome in the Collaborative Longitudinal Personality Disorders Study (CLPS), even though research on these categories remains thin.

SCHIZOTYPAL, SCHIZOID, AND PARANOID PDs

These three categories all lie on the schizophrenic spectrum and are associated with a family history of psychosis (Siever & Davis, 1991). The hybrid proposal in Section III of *DSM–5* folds them into a single category of schizotypal PD. However, they remain separate in Section II.

Gerald was a 27-year-old man who lived alone and was unemployed. He came to clinical attention after an altercation with the police, following a complaint that he had failed to clean up his yard. Gerald had never trusted people and had a vague feeling of threat around strangers. He had no friends and had never had an intimate relationship of any kind. He spent his days watching videos and sometimes went out to the mall. He was a visibly strange man, who rarely made eye contact, but Gerald did not complain that he felt lonely. In his mind, he simply marched to a different drummer.

This vignette is a typical example of schizotypal PD, characterized by social isolation and odd behaviors and thoughts. It is often considered a subclinical form of schizophrenia, but since patients with these diagnoses rarely go on to develop frank psychosis, even though schizotypal PD is cross-referenced in the schizophrenia section of *DSM–5*, it continues to be classified as a PD. This may or may not be a wise choice. For example, in earlier editions of *DSM*, a category called *cyclothymic personality* was considered a PD but was eventually moved to the bipolar section. The *ICD* system never considered schizotypal disorder to be a PD, and in the second edition of the *DSM*, a similar condition was called *simple schizophrenia*, that is, schizophrenia without overt psychotic symptoms.

Research on schizotypal PD shows that it shares biomarkers with schizophrenia. Both conditions show abnormal saccadic eye movements, which is a biomarker associated with psychosis, and neuroimaging findings are similar in both diagnoses as well (Chemerinski et al., 2013). What makes schizotypal patients different is outcome. In the CLPS (Gunderson et al., 2011), their symptoms had the same tendency seen in other PDs for improvement over time and did not progress to psychosis.

Schizoid PD is characterized by a lack of interest in social relationships and emotional coldness. In other words, it has features of schizotypy without resembling psychosis. However, the distinctions between schizoid and schizotypal PDs may only be a matter of degree. In fact, the *DSM–5* proposal in Section III eliminates schizoid PD, folding it into the schizotypal category.

Paranoid PD is characterized by pervasive, long-standing suspiciousness. The alternative model also folds it into schizotypal PD. This would have been a good decision, but implementation will have to wait for another edition of the *DSM*. As for community prevalence, the National Comorbidity Survey Replication (NCS–R; Lenzenweger, Lane, Loranger, & Kessler, 2007) found 3.3% for schizotypal, 4.9% for schizoid, and 2.3% for paranoid. However, some community surveys suggest differential heritability. Torgersen et al. (2000) reported a heritability of .61 for schizotypal, .29 for schizoid, and .28 for paranoid.

In clinical settings, these PDs are not common. Zimmerman et al. (2005) found a prevalence of 0.6% for schizotypal and 1.4% for schizoid; in the same study, 4.2% met criteria for paranoid PD. However, if patients with these diagnoses do not stay long in the mental health system, that might explain why so little research has been done on them.

The definitions of these categories are somewhat arbitrary and depend on clinical tradition. Although paranoid PD can be found in all editions of the manual, dating back to the first edition of the *DSM*, it has nine criteria, each of which describes suspiciousness in a different context. We are probably looking at a trait that lies on a continuum, not a disorder describing interactions between multiple trait dimensions.

HISTRIONIC PD

This category tells a story about the history of psychiatry. Decades ago, a category of *hysteria* was popular, used to describe a wide range of patients, some of whom had conversion or other somatic symptoms, and some of whom had personality traits associated with stimulus-seeking, high extraversion, and a dramatic style of communication (Scull, 2009). Eventually, hysteria disappeared from psychiatry and was split into several pieces, one of which was hysterical personality, a category seen in earlier editions of *DSM*. In the third edition of the *DSM*, (*DSM–III*) the disorder was renamed *histrionic* to emphasize the dramatic flair believed to characterize these patients. One of the criticisms often applied to this category is that it might reflect a gender bias (Funtowicz & Widiger, 1999). Diagnoses of histrionic PD are usually made in women, with seductiveness as a diagnostic criterion.

Typical cases of histrionic PD may occasionally be seen in the clinic, but after 50 years in *DSM*, it remains unsupported by research, so it was time to remove it from the manual, and its continued presence is a historical anomaly. There are also no data on treatment for histrionic PD. The Cochrane group has published a protocol for reviewing this literature (Stoffers, Ferriter, et al., 2012), but there were no systematic studies for them to review and was withdrawn in 2014.

AVOIDANT PD

Joy was a 28-year-old woman working in a call center. She could cope with this task, which gave her distance from difficult clients. She lived alone and spent weekends at the gym or doing photography. Joy had a few old friends but was too anxious about rejection to seek new ones. Joy would not accept invitations to parties or to other social events where she would have to chat with new people. However, when Joy remained single as her friends went on to marry and raise children, she felt lonely and left out of life.

This is a typical example of avoidant PD, a diagnosis introduced in *DSM–III* and that was a brainchild of the psychologist Theodore Millon. It describes patients who are socially anxious, and who, unlike patients with schizoid PD, desire relationships but are too afraid of rejection to take the chance of forming them. Torgersen et al. (2000) found the avoidant category to be the most common PD in Norway, with a prevalence of 5%, and the NCS–R (Lenzenweger et al., 2007) had exactly the same number. Not only are these patients common in the community, but Zimmerman et al. (2005) found that 14% of patients in a large psychiatric clinic met criteria for the diagnosis, much more than patients with a Cluster A diagnoses. Torgersen et al. (2000) found the heritability of this disorder to be .28, much lower than other disorders in Cluster C.

Avoidant PD has a large overlap with social anxiety disorder (Sanislow, da Cruz, Gianoli, & Reagan, 2012). Thus, the small literature on treatment, as reviewed by the Cochrane group (Ahmed et al., 2012), describes cognitive behavior therapy methods developed for social anxiety. There is no specific protocol for treating avoidant patients, and there have been no clinical trials, although it is possible that some of the methods developed for social anxiety are also effective in avoidant PD.

DEPENDENT PD

This category is defined in a way that might lead one to ask, "How many ways can people be overly dependent?" Like paranoid PD, it does not really describe a complex of traits, as in other PDs, but a single trait in multiple contexts. This is a heritable dimension, as shown by Torgersen et al. (2000), who found a coefficient of .57. Community prevalence is low, with Lenzenweger et al. (2007) reporting 0.6%, and clinical prevalence is only 1% (Zimmerman et al., 2005).

A research group led by Adelphi University psychologist Robert Bornstein (2005) has been consistently interested in dependent PD. His studies examine the consequences of dependent personality traits, which lead to difficulties later in life as social networks narrow. However, this literature remains thin (Disney, 2013). There is no specific protocol for treating dependent patients, and there have been no clinical trials.

OBSESSIVE–COMPULSIVE PD

William was a 37-year-old accountant, valued by his firm for precision and commitment. However, he often worked overtime to make sure he had done his job properly. This led to conflict with his wife, who found him emotionally unavailable, both to herself and to the children. The marriage was in a fragile state, but William could not see why. He made a good living, did not drink, and had never been unfaithful. He saw his wife as making unreasonable demands for attention that interfered with his personal space.

This is a typical example of obsessive–compulsive PD (OCPD). This category is another example of a pure trait disturbance that fades imperceptibly into normality. In terms of the five-factor model, it mainly describes high Conscientiousness (Widiger & Costa, 2013). OCPD was the most frequent PD identified in the National Epidemiologic Survey on Alcohol and Related Conditions Study, even when the data were reanalyzed by Trull et al. (2010). OCPD has attracted little other research, except for the CLPS (Gunderson et al., 2011), which showed that it improves with time. Its heritability is .78 (Torgersen et al., 2000). There is no specific protocol for treating patients with OCPD, and no clinical trials of any method of treatment. Because of their emotional rigidity, these patients do not always do well in standard psychotherapy, so one might consider developing specific protocols for OCPD, as well as conducting research on the efficacy of group or couple therapy.

PD, UNSPECIFIED

PD, not otherwise specified (now called PD, unspecified) is the most common PD clinicians see (Coccaro, Nayyer, & McCloskey, 2012; Verheul, Bartak, & Widiger, 2007). Zimmerman et al. (2005) found it in 14.1% of their sample. Any patient who meets overall criteria for a PD but does not meet criteria for any specific category will qualify for this category. Yet the diagnosis is not always made because the clinician must carefully follow the rules set down in *DSM–5*.

The question is whether this is a meaningful entity or a wastebasket. Patients meeting criteria for a PD can still be very different from each other. Putting them in the same category says more about problems in the *DSM* system than it does about clinical characteristics. The one common factor is that, like other PD patients, they suffer from psychosocial dysfunction, although symptoms are less severe than they are in specific PDs (Wilberg, Hummelen, Pedersen, & Karterud, 2008).

The 10 categories of PD, retained in *DSM–5*, generally do a poor job of describing the full range of psychopathology described by the PD construct as a whole. They are traditional labels that do not correspond to the factors identified by trait psychology. One of the innovations suggested in the model in Section III of *DSM–5* was to use trait dimensional profiles to classify these cases. This would have helped clinicians, and I hope this useful idea will eventually be revived.

THREE

TREATMENT

Psychopharmacology

This chapter reviews the evidence for the usefulness of medication for patients with personality disorders (PDs). By and large, there is no such evidence. Most patients with PD would be better off taking no medication at all. (The main exception is for managing symptoms such as severe insomnia.) Thus, clinical psychologists are not "missing" anything if they fail to obtain psychiatric consultation on their patients with PDs. Furthermore, because psychiatrists, once consulted, inevitably suggest a prescription, even when it is not evidence based, these procedures are likely to do patients a disservice. This is a sad story, in which my own profession of psychiatry has gone badly wrong, but as with any clinical error, it is important to understand why it has happened.

http://dx.doi.org/10.1037/14642-010
A Concise Guide to Personality Disorders, by J. Paris

WHY DRUGS ARE PRESCRIBED FOR
PATIENTS WITH PDs

Clinical practice in mental health is more and more dominated by psychopharmacology. Clinical psychologists do not prescribe drugs, but many of their patients receive them anyway. This is partly because physicians believe in their efficacy and partly because patients themselves, influenced by advertising and the media, insist on them. There is also pressure from insurance policies, which reward rapid assessments and pharmacological treatment methods.

I have written (Paris, 2010c) a detailed critique of the evidence for "aggressive" psychopharmacology. Medication is essential for severe mental disorders (schizophrenia, bipolar illness, melancholic depression). However, many drugs on the market are vastly overprescribed, and not just for patients with PDs. They are routinely given to patients with common mental disorders (anxiety, depression) who may receive only marginal benefit or no benefit from them at all.

A majority of the prescriptions for psychiatric drugs are now being written by primary care physicians. Seven percent of all patient visits to a family doctor lead to treatment with one or more of these agents (Mojtabai & Olfson, 2011). The frequency of these prescriptions has doubled in part because patients are now being given antidepressants on a long-term basis (Moore et al., 2009) but also because pharmacological intervention has become a knee-jerk reaction for physicians. The prevalence of antidepressant prescriptions now exceeds the prevalence of depression itself (Mojtabai & Olfson, 2011), showing that these drugs are being prescribed for distress rather than for treatment of specific diagnoses. Given the comorbidity between depression and PD, many patients with PD will receive antidepressants, even though their efficacy in this population is doubtful at best (Newton-Howes, Tyrer, & Johnson, 2006).

These observations raise questions about whether patients would benefit if clinical psychologists, who treat so many depressed patients, should gain prescribing privileges. Many in the profession have supported this proposal (McGrath, 2010). However, I would not like to see this happen. My views have nothing to do with defending a medical guild and everything to do with protecting patients from unnecessary treatment.

Today, 11% of the population is taking antidepressants (Pratt, Brody, & Gu, 2011). If psychologists, who outnumber most other mental health professionals, begin to prescribe these agents, the current rate of use would probably increase even further. Nonmedical health professionals would be as reluctant as physicians are to "take the chance" of failing to write a prescription. McGrath (2010) acknowledged this possibility but downplayed it. To be fair, we do not actually know how this scenario would play out, but the current climate is one in which patients expect pharmacological intervention. I worry that psychologists, once allowed to prescribe, would be under enormous pressure to do so, at much the same rate as physicians. They would also make more money, while the problem of overdiagnosis and overprescription could become even worse than it is today.

Another concern is that psychiatrists' sharply declining use of psychotherapy (Mojtabai & Olfson, 2008) would spread to clinical psychology. I am concerned that the most skilled therapists in the mental health system will stop doing what they do best and end up carrying out the same mindless treatment that currently afflicts psychiatry. This would constitute a serious threat to public health. It is already the case that clinical psychologists feel required to obtain a medical consultation to protect themselves against any criticism that antidepressants have not been prescribed. When patients are not doing well, referrals to physicians become even more common. If psychologists prescribed, it would be difficult for them to resist patients' demands for drugs, and they might well be seduced by the increased income that is possible when professionals see more patients for briefer appointments rather than spend an hour conducting a psychotherapy session.

Thus, the problem with the overuse of psychopharmacology does not depend on professional discipline. It is rooted in a widespread belief that mentally troubled people cannot be treated successfully without drugs. Although there is no doubt that pharmacological agents are essential for patients with psychoses and severe depression, their efficacy for common mental disorders, such as mild to moderate depression, is often hardly better than a placebo (Kirsch et al., 2008).

The belief that psychologically troubled patients must receive pharmacological treatment has become part of both our medical culture and the wider culture, replacing the older idea that everybody should be in psychotherapy. When psychologists ask for consultations on their patients from psychiatrists because they are afraid of missing an indication for drugs, the result is guaranteed. A consultant feels required to suggest something. If the first agent tried is not effective, patients end up trying at least one more drug, if not several more, and often in combination. Yet as shown by effectiveness research (Valenstein, 2006), the benefits of antidepressants have strikingly diminished returns when physicians switch from one drug to another or carry out augmentation strategies with additional drugs.

PDs reflect complex problems and have effects on work and interpersonal relationships. Reducing them to symptoms, especially mood symptoms, almost always misses the point. So how do psychiatrists, who should know better, get this so wrong? By invoking the concept of "comorbidity," they are not treating the patient as a whole but aiming only for symptom relief. Unfortunately, this often means treating every symptom with a different drug. So beware of psychiatrists who speak of comorbidity; they already have pen in hand waiting to write a prescription, whether for depression, anxiety, or putative attention-deficit/hyperactivity disorder. This unhappy scenario plays out all too often in patients with PDs.

PSYCHOPHARMACOLOGY FOR PDs

The evidence that psychopharmacological agents are effective in the treatment of PDs is weak. Most of the research has concerned borderline PD (BPD), and there is a Cochrane report summarizing the evidence (Stoffers et al., 2010). The best that can be said is that drugs that are sedating have a temporary calming effect on agitation, but patients with BPD have comorbid symptoms of depression, mood instability, and impulsivity, and thus the temptation to prescribe agents targeted for those problems often proves irresistible. That aggressive pharmacological treatment and polypharmacy have become the rule in BPD is well documented (Zanarini, Frankenburg, Khera, & Bleichmar, 2001). The situation has only gotten worse since the article by Zanarini et al. was published in 2001.

Most of my colleagues continue to prescribe in this way, even those who have done research on PDs and should know better. When I question them on the subject, they respond that the patients they see are too sick for psychotherapy. In other words, they feel they have to do *something*, and who knows whether another drug might not work? Moreover, experts in PD research are not always skilled in psychological treatments and may be reluctant to obtain access to therapists who are.

I am particularly critical of the practice of polypharmacy, which is not at all evidence based; no clinical trials on drug combinations for PDs have been conducted. To prescribe five drugs to one patient suggests an absence of judgment and understanding. Mental illness is not a set of symptoms, each of which needs a separate magic bullet. Actually, providing a different drug for each symptom is not a new phenomenon in medical practice. This is an approach that the famous physician William Osler (1898) described over a century ago as "shotgun medicine."

I am painting a grim picture, but it corresponds to the way psychiatry is currently being practiced. I spend much of my own time in a treatment team for PDs getting patients *off* medication and ensuring they receive evidence-based psychotherapy. By and large, PD patients are better if they take nothing at all. I would now like to examine the empirical evidence behind these conclusions.

Antidepressants

Even in depressions not complicated by a PD, one sees only a small advantage of drug over placebo, with effects most marked in severe depressions (Kirsch et al., 2008). Yet because patients with BPD are often comorbid for dysthymia or major depression (Zanarini et al., 1998), they are frequently offered antidepressants. Consistent evidence shows that the presence of *any* PD makes drug treatment of depression much less effective (Newton-Howes et al., 2006). This is the real meaning of *treatment-resistant depression*. In a

Cochrane review, Stoffers et al. (2010) found no clinical trials supporting the use of antidepressants in BPD. The National Institute of Clinical Excellence guidelines in the United Kingdom did not recommend them at all (Kendall, Burbeck, & Bateman, 2010). Fortunately, these agents do little harm. So when I reduce previously prescribed medication, I usually leave antidepressants for last.

Tricyclics were the first drugs to be widely used for depression. The problem with prescribing them for patients with PD who are chronically suicidal is that taking a week's supply can be fatal. Moreover, tricyclics have anticholinergic side effect profiles that often lead to noncompliance. Similar concerns about the danger of overdose arise for monoamine oxidase inhibitors, and patients may fail to follow the dietary restrictions that are required to avoid hypertension. These drugs are rarely used today for PD patients.

Because selective serotonin reuptake inhibitors (SSRIs) are much safer, they have been widely used, especially in BPD. However clinical trials suggest that their efficacy is limited. By and large, SSRIs have more consistent effects on aggression and anger than on depression or mood swings (Kendall et al., 2010). Antidepressants temporarily "take the edge off" and are also sedating enough to reduce anxiety. That can be useful, but one never sees remission of the PD.

Mood Stabilizers

BPD is associated with marked affective instability (Koenigsberg, 2010) or emotion dysregulation (Linehan, 1993). Patients show rapid mood swings and do not easily calm down once upset. The idea that affective instability lies in the bipolar spectrum is not supported by research (Paris, 2012), nor does research support the idea that BPD is a form of bipolarity (Paris, Gunderson, & Weinberg, 2007). This helps explain why mood stabilizers—lithium and antiepileptic agents—do not produce a remission in BPD, as they often do in bipolar I and bipolar II disorders. The idea that BPD patients with emotion dysregulation benefit from these agents is not based on evidence but derives from the misleading term *mood stabilizer*. However, as with SSRIs, mood stabilizers that are sedating often yield some reduction in anger and aggression. Claims that mood stabilizers have a larger effect on impulsivity than either SSRIs or antipsychotics (Ingenhoven, Lafay, Rinne, Passchier, & Duivenvoorden, 2010) are misleading, given that the meta-analyses on which these conclusions are based include randomized controlled trials (RCTs) with small samples and dubious methodologies.

It is not surprising that mood stabilizers have, at best, only a partial effect in BPD. If affective instability arises from entirely different pathological mechanisms from bipolar disorder, then these symptoms may require entirely different drugs that have yet to be developed. If and when they are invented, I will be happy to prescribe them.

Antipsychotics

Antipsychotics, usually in low doses, have long been used in BPD. However typical neuroleptics have many troubling side effects, particularly when used long-term, and clinical guidelines have specifically warned against using them in PDs (Kendall, Burbeck, & Bateman, 2010). The development of atypical neuroleptics, which are better tolerated, has made the prescription of antipsychotics much more common. However, these agents have a serious side effect, one that develops after patients are under treatment for several months: a metabolic syndrome associated with weight gain and diabetes (Newcomer & Haupt, 2006). This is a good reason for caution in prescribing these agents and for quickly discontinuing them once administered.

Atypical antipsychotics are effective for the psychotic symptoms that accompany BPD (Rosenbluth & Sinyor, 2012). Yet once again, their main effects on BPD are a reduction in impulsivity and anger, without remission of the disorder. Nonetheless, short-term use can be of benefit. The problem is that once the patient is on an antipsychotic, physicians are afraid to discontinue it, but the longer patients take antipsychotics, they more side effects they will have. Add to that the high doses of atypical antipsychotics that physicians sometimes prescribe when patients do not have an initial response.

Most clinical trials thus far have been conducted on olanzapine, all of which were sponsored by Eli Lilly (the company that manufactures this agent). Yet perhaps the most common drug used in practice these days is quetiapine, which thus far has only one short-term clinical trial in BPD (Black et al., 2014). This agent may be preferred because it is a little less likely to cause weight gain and metabolic syndrome. Another popular alternative is aripiprazole, which has never been tested systematically in BPD.

Overall, the effects of neuroleptics are occasionally useful but usually marginal. Given their side effects, they should only be used on a short-term basis.

Polypharmacy

When patients show a short-term improvement after being prescribed a drug but the improvement does not last, there can be several possible explanations. One is that the original response was a placebo effect that had to be temporary. Another is that a drug can be sedating in a state of great agitation but did not affect any of the other symptoms of a disorder. Then this scenario can lead to the prescription of additional drugs, usually by adding a new agent (without subtracting what the patient is already taking). This sequence helps explain why so many BPD patients are on a polypharmacy regime of four or five drugs (Zanarini et al., 2001), with at least one agent from each major group.

For some time there have been published algorithms for drug treatment of various conditions, suggesting a sequence of prescriptions, each of which would target different symptoms. The American Psychiatric Association (2001) guidelines for BPD, now out of date, were deeply flawed from the beginning because they adopted this approach, doing real damage to practice by offering algorithms for pharmacotherapy that were not based on RCTs, which carried a heavy burden of side effects, and guaranteed polypharmacy. The more conservative conclusions of the National Institute for Clinical Excellence (Kendall et al., 2010) in the United Kingdom recommended that drugs should be prescribed with great caution in BPD.

In summary, drugs for BPD are nonspecific stopgaps with limited value that could eventually be replaced by better and more precise alternatives. We do not have agents that specifically target the traits that underlie BPD: impulsivity and affective instability. If we had an effective pharmacological treatment for these trait dimensions, psychiatry would be revolutionized.

There is even less evidence for prescribing drugs for other PDs. However, there may be a benefit in using low-dose antipsychotics for schizotypal PD (Chemerinski, Triebwasser, Roussos, & Siever, 2013).

What is discouraging about current practice is that drugs are being given to patients with PDs only because psychotherapy is not available. If these agents are used, we need to apply the same principles for evaluating them as for any medical illness—that is, a number of RCTs that is sufficient to conduct meta-analyses that yield replicable findings. These are the standards of reports by the Cochrane group, the most reliable and comprehensive source of information about the efficacy of pharmacological and psychotherapeutic treatments. Cochrane's conclusions about efficacy in BPD (Stoffers et al., 2010) were typically cautious and tentative. The existing literature, marked by small samples, short follow-up periods, and lack of replication, does not meet accepted standards. Drugs for PDs do not have any effect on personality pathology, and most have potentially serious somatic side effects. We need to consider alternatives—that is, the forms of psychotherapy that have been specifically developed for PDs. That is the subject of the next chapter.

10

Psychotherapies

Psychotherapy for personality disorders (PDs), like any other form of treatment, should be evidence based. For many years, if you wanted to read about treatment, the only choices you had were to read books describing the clinical experience of an "expert." You could also go to workshops to learn about these ideas. Recommendations were not based on empirical evidence, however, because there wasn't any.

Almost all research on the treatment of PDs has studied patients meeting criteria for borderline PD (BPD), which is also the condition that most interests clinicians. Starting with the seminal work of Linehan (1993), a number of innovative methods of treatment have been tested in clinical trials and shown to be effective. There are now half a dozen therapies for patients with BPD, each described by an acronym. I am not convinced, however, that they work in different ways and have different effects.

http://dx.doi.org/10.1037/14642-011
A Concise Guide to Personality Disorders, by J. Paris

Three caveats should be considered. First, even if one follows a tested method of psychotherapy, many decisions still need to be made that derive from experience and skill. Second, research on the therapy of BPD does not have the heft of literature on other mental disorders, such as depression or anxiety. Third, there is no evidence that any one method that has been tested is better than any other. Any therapy that is well planned will be better than unstructured treatment as usual (TAU) because it provides patients with external structures that make up for their inner chaos.

A further limitation, one that applies to any psychotherapy, is that not every patient can be expected to benefit from treatment. Even in the most seriously ill, however, rehabilitation can have partial effects. Yet some are sicker than others, and those who do best usually have "ego strengths"— a job, an intimate relationship, or both. These areas of positive functioning provide patients with a base on which to build skills in other areas. Although there are always surprises and some patients who are seriously ill may recover, the observation that better functioning is predictive of outcome in psychotherapy is a well-known and consistent finding in research (Bohart & Greaves-Wade, 2013). If you are treating patients who have no job, no relationship, and no life to speak of, what is there to work on? If, on the other hand, patients have a life, then therapy benefits from a laboratory setting in which people can practice what they learn in treatment sessions.

Although specialized therapies may not be different from each other, not all psychotherapies applied in practice are equal. What researchers call TAU tends to be a mess in which patients talk about their problems to a sympathetic professional but are not given specific guidance in overcoming dysfunctional emotions, thoughts, and behaviors. This is why clinical trials always find that specific methods do better than TAU: It is not hard to do better. Yet when comparisons are made between two well-structured approaches, differences usually disappear (McMain et al., 2009; Zanarini, 2009). Patients need planned and structured forms of therapy, but the brand name may make no difference.

SPECIFIC METHODS OF PSYCHOTHERAPY FOR BPD

Dialectical Behavior Therapy

Dialectical behavior therapy (DBT) was the first evidence-based treatment for BPD. Developed by Marsha Linehan (1993), this was the first psychotherapy for BPD to undergo successful clinical trials (Linehan, Armstrong, Suarez, Allmon, & Heard, 1991; Linehan et al., 2006). The introduction of DBT was a turning point in the treatment of the disorder, and its principles lie at the core of all successful therapy in this population. Here, at last, was a practical approach that targeted the key traits and symptoms of BPD.

Today, DBT remains the leading evidence-based method of therapy for patients with BPD. It is an adaptation of cognitive behavioral therapy (CBT), combined with interventions common to other approaches, but specifically designed to target the emotion dysregulation that characterizes BPD, and to reduce impulsive behaviors. It applies *chain analysis* to incidents leading to self-injury and overdoses—that is, showing patients what emotions lead up to impulsive behaviors and teaching them alternative ways of handling dysphoric emotions. DBT also emphasizes empathic responses to distress that provide validation for the inner experience of patients. The program consists of weekly individual therapy, group psychoeducation, telephone availability for coaching, as well as support through consultation for therapists undertaking these procedures. The method is an eclectic mix of behavior therapy, CBT, mindfulness based on Zen Buddhism, and original ideas such as *radical acceptance* (Linehan, 1993). These techniques have been described in some detail (Linehan, 2014; Linehan & Koerner, 2012).

The first published trial (Linehan et al., 1991) compared 1 year of DBT with TAU and found DBT to be superior, especially in regard to reductions in self-harm, overdose, and hospitalization. The question was whether it was too easy to do better than TAU. For this reason, Linehan et al. (2006) conducted a second clinical trial in which the comparison group was "treatment by community experts"—therapists who identified themselves as interested in BPD and experienced in its treatment. The results again favored DBT, with reductions in overdoses and subsequent hospitalizations within a year, although this time there were no differences between the groups in the frequency of self-harm. Replication studies in other centers produced similar results, albeit with higher rates of attrition (Linehan & Koerner, 2012). A meta-analysis (Kliem, Kröger, & Kosfelder, 2010) supported the conclusion that DBT is an effective and specific method that is superior to traditional ways of treating BPD patients.

Although several specific methods of therapy designed for BPD symptoms have been supported by randomized controlled trials (Paris, 2010b), the strongest evidence supports DBT. The method is a clinical application of psychological research on emotion regulation (Gross, 2013). The dysregulation in BPD leads to unstable emotions that are abnormal responses to interpersonal conflict (Koenigsberg, 2010). That conclusion has been confirmed by studies of BPD patients using ecological momentary assessment, a technology that allows researchers to track emotional instability more closely by immediate recording of affective and behavioral responses to life events (Russell et al., 2007; Trull et al., 2008). In DBT, patients are taught better ways of calming down, during and after emotional storms, which then reduces the frequency of self-harm and overdoses.

There are some important unanswered questions about DBT. Although the original cohort received therapy 20 years ago, it has never been followed up, so we do not know whether treated samples maintain their gains and continue to improve beyond a 1-year posttreatment follow-up. Also, given the resources required to conduct DBT, it needs to be determined whether this complex program can be dismantled or streamlined for greater clinical impact. One report found that a 6-month version of the therapy can also be effective (Stanley, Brodsky, Nelson, & Dulit, 2007). A treatment lasting for a year (and often more) becomes quickly inaccessible as waiting lists grow and most patients and their families cannot afford the expense.

Finally, there is the question of whether DBT is a uniquely efficacious treatment for BPD or whether other well-structured approaches can produce the same results. To address this issue, McMain et al. (2009)

administered DBT for 1 year, with random assignment to a comparison condition called *general psychiatric management*, a manualized version of the American Psychiatric Association (2001) guidelines for the treatment of BPD. The results of this comparative trial found no differences between the groups in overdoses, hospitalization, or self-harm. This negative finding had important clinical implications. It suggests that although DBT is better than most treatments, it can be matched by other therapies that are designed for this population and that are equally well-structured. Further, because results were good in both groups, the treatment package used for the comparison has now been studied on its own, under the name of *good psychiatric management* (Gunderson & Links, 2014).

A key question about DBT is whether the results of the treatment are specific to the method or to the structure. By and large, psychotherapy research supports a common factors model in which all well-structured treatments yield similar outcomes (Wampold, 2001). The positive results of DBT could be due to its high level of structure rather than to its specific interventions. This supposition was supported by the study by McMain et al. (2009). So although DBT is clearly better than TAU and somewhat better than treatment by therapists with experience in treating BPD, it is not necessarily better than a well-thought-out program of clinical management.

The popularity of DBT depends on its comprehensiveness, as well as on its commitment to conducting research to demonstrate its efficacy. DBT is not the only evidence-based therapy on the market, but it is the only method that has been tested in multiple clinical trials outside the center where it was developed, showing that its efficacy cannot be accounted for by allegiance effects. The ideas behind DBT are fundamental for any therapist seeing patients with BPD. It is not a narrowly focused form of treatment that only deals with cognitive schemata; it also provides validating responses to current emotional upsets and offers education about emotion regulation.

However, there is a serious problem with DBT: Its expense makes it inaccessible. This is mainly because of the length of therapy. DBT has been tested for a year, but even that length of time is beyond most insurance policies or the financial resources of most families. Of even more concern, Linehan (1993) suggested that even this lengthy period may be only the first phase of a treatment that could go on for several years. I am reminded of the story of psychoanalysis in which inevitably incomplete results led to an interminable course of therapy. DBT is effective but is accessible only to those who can pay for it. Even if it were properly insured, its length would still make access a problem: Clinics offering the treatment, even for 12 months, often have extensive waiting lists. It is important to shorten DBT or to make it intermittent (or do both). This is the only way to provide service to more patients.

We all owe a debt to Marsha Linehan. I have learned an enormous amount from her and have applied her principles in all the clinics I lead that treat BPD. Moreover, Linehan's recent public statements, acknowledging that she herself once suffered from BPD but recovered, were courageous and have done a great deal to reduce the stigma associated with this disorder. Nonetheless, treatment for BPD suffers from the perception that DBT is the only brand that works. Therapists should not feel badly if they are not in a position to provide DBT in a formal way or to refer patients to a DBT clinic. In the next chapter, I show that its principles can be incorporated into normal clinical practice. In my view, brand names are bad for therapy. As cognitive theory evolves, it has become a more general term for what might be called simply *psychotherapy* (Beck & Haigh, 2014). Livesley (2012) recommended that DBT give up its brand name and incorporate its best ideas into a general model of treatment for BPD.

Other Evidence-Based Psychotherapies for BPD

Although other methods have been devised, they do not differ from DBT in any essential way (Paris, in press). We now examine those that have undergone clinical trials.

Mentalization-based treatment (MBT; Bateman & Fonagy, 2006) is rooted in attachment theory, but the method also has a strong cognitive component. Its assumption is that BPD patients have trouble recognizing emotions (their own and those of other people), that is, *mentalization.*

MBT teaches patients how to do that better. Like most effective programs, it uses a combination of group and individual therapy. Although developed by psychoanalysts, it uses a number of cognitive methods similar to DBT in that patients are taught to recognize their emotions, learn how to tolerate them, and manage them in more adaptive ways.

MBT was first tested in a randomized controlled trial (RCT) in a day program lasting 18 months (Bateman & Fonagy, 2001) and found to be superior to TAU. A second study in a larger sample of outpatients given 18 months of treatment found a decline of both self-reported symptoms and clinically significant problems, including suicide attempts and hospitalization (Bateman & Fonagy, 2009). This is the only method for which researchers have followed up a cohort for 8 years to determine if the effects of treatment remain stable, which turned out to be the case (Bateman & Fonagy, 2004).

MBT needs successful clinical trials in centers outside the hospital where it originated. Thus far, the only attempt at replication outside the United Kingdom reported few differences from standard therapy (Jørgensen et al., 2013). However, Bateman and Fonagy (2008) do not consider MBT as a "one-and-only" approach but encourage mental health workers to learn its principles and then apply them in their own clinical settings, without necessarily following a strict protocol. One can only applaud such open-mindedness and flexibility. Finally, Bateman and Fonagy (2008) have stated that the results of their research are not specific to their method but support any structured approach to psychotherapy. This may be the most consistent finding in this literature (Choi-Kain & Gunderson, 2008).

Transference-focused psychotherapy (TFP; Clarkin, Levy, Lenzenweger, & Kernberg, 2007) is based on the theories of the psychoanalyst Otto Kernberg. It differs from other methods in that its focus is on distortions between therapist and patient in the session, used to illustrate interpersonal problems elsewhere in the patient's life. It has thus far undergone two clinical trials, one comparing it with DBT, with only minimal differences (Clarkin, Levy, Lenzenweger, & Kernberg, 2007), and one comparing it with TAU, to which it was superior (Doering et al., 2010). TFP aims to generalize what happens in therapy to outside relationships.

Given the long record of failure for psychodynamic therapy in BPD, one might consider this approach with caution. Nonetheless, at this point TFP has about as much support as MBT. It shares the advantage of being structured and well thought out.

Cognitive analytic therapy is based on similar concepts and can be considered as another psychodynamic–cognitive hybrid. It applies object relations theory to establish a firmer sense of self in patients. It has been tested in a population of adolescents (Chanen & McCutcheon, 2013), where it was effective, albeit not superior, to a manualized version of "good clinical care."

Schema-focused therapy (SFT; Young, Klosko, & Weishaar, 2003) is another mixture of cognitive and psychodynamic approaches that aims to modify how patients think about their world (i.e., cognitive schemata), but it also focuses on the distorting effects of negative childhood experiences. It has undergone one clinical trial comparing it with transference-focused psychotherapy (Giesen-Bloo et al., 2006), with only minor differences in outcome and one trial in which it was superior to TAU (Bamelis, Evers, Spinhoven, & Arntz, 2014). The problem with schema-focused therapy is that it is designed to last for 3 years, making it even more inaccessible than DBT.

Standard CBT has been tested in a study conducted in the United Kingdom (Davidson, Tyrer, Norrie, Palmer, & Tyrer, 2010). After an average of 26 sessions, BPD patients did better with cognitive therapy than with TAU. It also seems likely that CBT for BPD is now being conducted on broader, more flexible principles. When a Cochrane review (Stoffers, Völlm, et al., 2012) concluded that the data for cognitive therapy were "promising," they were not thinking of standard CBT. Linehan had developed DBT because of her impression that standard CBT was not effective for BPD. Yet a large RCT (Davidson et al., 2010) found manualized CBT, modified to target PD symptoms, was superior to TAU for the treatment of recurrent deliberate self-harm.

It is important to know that therapy lasting for a few months can be effective. The evidence for this conclusion was recently reviewed by Davidson and Tran (2014). What was most striking about these findings was that the mean length of treatment was 16 sessions. This suggests that BPD might be treated more rapidly, and less expensively, than by treatments designed to continue for a year or two. Perhaps the most chronic and severe patients with BPD require several years of therapy, but it makes no sense to make a long duration the standard of care.

Systems training for emotional predictability and problem solving (STEPPS; Blum et al., 2008) is a brief and practical program that closely resembles DBT in its focus on emotion regulation skills. It is designed to supplement TAU, particularly in settings where specialized individual therapies are not available. STEPPS, based on psychoeducation in groups, has been supported by clinical trials, with a 1-year follow-up (Blum et al., 2008).

STEPPS is a short-term intervention with psychoeducation conducted in groups, designed to supplement standard psychotherapy or management conducted elsewhere. It is particularly suitable for populations living in regions where specialized treatment is not available. It is inexpensive and offers ready accessibility. STEPPS has been subjected to a successful clinical trial in BPD (Blum et al., 2008), with one replication (Bos, van der Wel, Appelo, & Verbraak, 2010). It has also undergone one test in the treatment of antisocial PD (Black, Gunter, Loveless, Allen, & Sieleni, 2010), although one cannot conclude that this makes antisocial PD as treatable as BPD.

COMMON FACTORS IN THE TREATMENT OF BPD

Although these individual approaches each have useful ideas and techniques, they work through common mechanisms (Paris, in press). A vast literature shows that the effective factors for outcome in any form of psychotherapy are common rather than specific (Wampold, 2001). Nor is it necessarily true that patients with BPD can only be seen in specialized clinics; most benefit from what Gunderson and Links (2014) termed *good psychiatric management*. The ideas behind effective therapy are spreading to the wider therapeutic community, and interventions (e.g., teaching emotion regulation) are becoming part of the armamentarium of therapists of all persuasions.

It is unfortunate that psychotherapy as a field continues to be defined by competing methods, many of which use a three-letter acronym. It is even more unfortunate that clinicians define themselves as practitioners of any single method. Research can help us get beyond these unnecessary divisions.

Thus, I agree with Livesley (2012), who suggests that psychotherapy should be evidence based, not acronym based. Even if some interventions are partly specific to BPD, we need a single model of therapy to make use of the best ideas for all sources. To have multiple methods competing for market share may be good for book sales, but it is not the way to develop evidence-based practice.

We do not need so many forms of psychotherapy, most of which resemble each other more in practice than in theory. If therapies based on so many different ideas and using many different techniques can produce the same results, they must have a lot in common. One of the main ingredients is structure. Traditional therapies for PD failed because they rely on unstructured techniques that leave patients adrift. These are not patients who get better just by being heard and supported. People with BPD also need specific instruction about emotion regulation, control of impulsivity, and life skills that can be used to find a job and build a social network.

Although different methods seem to target different aspects of PD, the failure of comparative trials to find large differences in outcome also suggests that common factors are of crucial importance. Again, consider the large body of research supporting the view that common factors (also called nonspecific factors) are the best predictors of results in all forms of psychotherapy (Wampold, 2001). By and large, when different forms of therapy are compared head to head, researchers almost always find equivalent results. The most important common factors are a strong working alliance, empathy, and a practical problem-solving approach to life problems (Baldwin & Imel, 2013; Crits-Christoph, Gibbons, & Mukherjee, 2013).

With a complex and challenging disorder like BPD, psychotherapy needs to maximize these mechanisms and find ways to make them more specific. The best-validated methods offer a defined structure, focus on the regulation of emotions, and encourage the solution of interpersonal problems through self-observation. Empathy and validation are essential elements of any therapy but are particularly important for BPD patients, many of whom are sensitive to the slightest hint of invalidation (Kohut, 1970; Linehan, 1993). In other words, these are patients who can easily feel that their emotions are being dismissed. They will not listen to anything else you have to say unless they perceive that their feelings are accepted.

Self-observation is a skill that therapists need to teach all their patients. When one learns to know feelings better (and not be derailed by them), one can stand aside from emotional crises or even begin to think about alternative solutions to problems. Clinicians who provide treatment following these principles do not necessarily need to refer patients to specialized programs.

IMPORTANCE OF STRUCTURE IN PSYCHOTHERAPY

Psychotherapy is the backbone of treatment in BPD, but clinicians in the past were not trained to apply structure to treatment sessions. That is probably why open-ended therapies have been associated with large dropout rates (Skodol, Buckley, & Charles, 1983). Moreover, therapies that focus too much on the past have a way of encouraging patients to regress.

The key to recovery from a PD is to "get a life." That usually means finding a job or going back to school to prepare for a job. Without a social role, recovery from a PD is less likely (Zanarini et al., 2012). Unfortunately, some of our patients make the mistake of trying to solve their life problems through an intimate relationship that gives the illusion, for a time, of unconditional love. In the absence of work, that strategy only makes them dependent on another person, seriously impeding self-mastery.

Finally, because PDs usually improve with time, therapy aims to hasten naturalistic recovery. Because patients can get better on their own, determining whether change is the result of a specific intervention requires testing through RCTs. Thus far, these trials have provided strong support for a few psychotherapy methods and tentative support for others.

In summary, even if a well-structured approach works well for most patients, generalized methods might be enough, and patients with BPD have done much better since DBT and other methods specific to the disorder were developed. We await the day when effective packages of this kind can be developed for other PDs.

WHAT WORKS, WHAT DOESN'T WORK, AND WHY

Because of their prominent mood symptoms, patients with BPD are often put on medication and can end up being prescribed four or five different drugs (Zanarini, Frankenburg, Khera, & Bleichmar, 2001). The review in Chapter 9 showed that these practices are not evidence based. The role of pharmacology in BPD treatment is limited and is most effective for short-term management of insomnia. Because most medications in current use (antipsychotics, antidepressants, and mood stabilizers) are sedating, they can "take the edge off" BPD symptoms through nonspecific effects on impulsivity. However, as shown by the most recent Cochrane report (Stoffers, Völlm, et al., 2012), none of these agents have specific effects on BPD itself. Most patients can be managed with minimal medication or with no medication at all.

Clinical psychologists treating BPD patients should therefore be cautious about obtaining psychopharmacological consults to "cover themselves." I understand why this happens; these are difficult, scary cases. However, when you ask for a consult with an MD, your patient may be put on an aggressive drug regime. If you read the literature, with its conservative conclusions, it will become clear that although drugs are palliative in the short term, no pharmacological agent produces remission in BPD. If you need consultation on difficult cases, I suggest you choose clinicians with expertise in the psychotherapy of BPD.

It must be acknowledged that psychotherapy for these patients has not always had a good reputation. More than 75 years ago, Stern (1938) described BPD as treatment-resistant (i.e., it didn't respond to psychoanalysis). Ever since, therapists have struggled with the obstacles the disorder presents. It is not easy to manage people who don't follow your advice, don't always come to appointments, and frequently threaten suicide.

Even so, many problems can also be understood as artifacts of well-meaning but insufficiently structured therapy. TAU is often the comparison point in research studies, but it might be better described as "the usual mess." Patients with BPD don't fit well into normal practice, in either clinics or offices. They need therapists trained to provide more specific interventions.

Yet even when therapy is based on a theory, it can still falter. In the past, patients with BPD were offered regressive psychoanalytic approaches that were unproductive or counterproductive. In BPD, therapy fails when too much time is spent talking about the past. Of course, if childhood was marked by trauma, life histories need to be validated and understood, but patients need to move on and deal with their current problems in relationships and work.

Standard methods of behavioral therapy and CBT may also run into difficulties in this population. Linehan (1993) developed DBT because standard CBT did not seem to be effective for treatment of BPD. For example, patients with BPD are not always willing to do the homework that CBT requires. Linehan's discovery was that therapy works best when offering specific strategies for emotion regulation. This was the great breakthrough that has made BPD a treatable disorder.

Moreover, the "supportive" techniques used in TAU (sessions that review the week and provide nonspecific encouragement) are not evidence based. Research on therapy for BPD shows that almost any specific method is better than TAU, underlining the limitations inherent in the reality of all these "usual" clinical practices. Yet, as more therapists become aware of more specific methods, TAU itself may be changing for the better.

Being an effective therapist for these patients may not depend that much on your theory about BPD. It is more important to understand people whose communication style can be difficult and problematic, to be comfortable with knowing that you cannot prevent suicide. If you want to treat BPD, the first requirement is a thick skin.

Yet psychotherapies designed for BPD have a stronger evidence base than any form of pharmacotherapy. As noted earlier, medications have never been shown to lead to the sustained remissions documented for psychological treatments. However, not "any old" psychotherapy will do. In the past, mistaken methods leading to poor results have given therapy for patients with BPD a difficult reputation.

Although no research has specifically examined TAU, it is not difficult to see why it doesn't work. Patients come to their sessions and tell stories about stressful events that have occurred over the week. Therapists validate feelings, but by itself, that does little for patients who misunderstand and distort their interpersonal environment. The danger is that patients will perceive that their therapists agree with them—that other people are to blame and that they are victims.

Empathy has to be linked to tactful confrontations to help patients learn new ways of understanding and dealing with problems, what Bateman and Fonagy (2006) called the *capacity to mentalize* (similar to the concept of mindfulness). Thus, using what Linehan (1993) called a *dialectical* approach, one must validate as one teaches new skills. The absence of such an approach is why supportive therapy has limited value. The aim must be to have a strong enough alliance with patients that they are willing to see their problems in a different light.

These principles help us to understand why classical psychodynamic therapy was often ineffective for BPD. Patients who cannot mentalize and who are constantly in the throes of emotion dysregulation cannot make use of procedures such as free association with a relatively silent therapist who only intervenes to make "interpretations." Moreover, when therapy focuses on the past rather than the present, patients are more likely to be mired down in their grievances than to move on (this is what Linehan meant by *radical acceptance*). People move on more easily when they feel understood, independent of a therapist's theories (Strupp, Fox, & Lesser, 1969). Reexperiencing traumatic events from childhood can be particularly counterproductive. A neuroimaging study helps to show why. Koenigsberg (2010) found that patients with BPD do not habituate to stressful thoughts but become increasingly activated and disturbed. Thus, therapies that focus on trauma produce regression and increase symptom levels.

In summary, therapies that are present oriented, have a strong cognitive component, balance acceptance and change, offer a predictable structure, and in which therapists are active and engaged are most likely to succeed. We need to place more importance on the present than the past to help patients to get a life. In most cases this means getting a job or an education. It can also mean raising a family. For some people, it may involve hobbies or volunteer work. In whatever form, one must engage with the world to get better. Patients also need to be told that they have to work on getting a life now, not wait for therapy to somehow make doing so easier.

INTEGRATED BPD TREATMENT

Although evidence-based treatments for BPD have emerged from specialized treatment programs, these clinics tend to be too expensive or inaccessible. Yet even though these are not the settings where most therapists work, the same principles can be applied to ordinary practice.

An example is the use of group therapy to teach patients behavioral and cognitive skills, which is part of the package offered by the methods that have been most systematically tested. Most clinicians in practice do not carry out this kind of treatment. This is why the STEPPS program was developed: to augment individual therapies conducted by therapists in the community by providing a group setting based on the principles of psychoeducation. Yet because few communities have access to STEPPS, therapists should consider doing more group therapy in their own practices or in group practices. Another example is the use of psychoeducation to teach life skills and emotion management. CBT has been doing this for decades. These methods can also be transferred to the setting of individual therapy.

Another implication of research on BPD treatment is that therapists need to move out of the primarily receptive mode they may have been taught to adopt. There is no contradiction between empathic listening and therapeutic activity.

Psychotherapy for BPD is being held back by the existence of multiple competing methods, each with a three-letter acronym. The results of these methods tend to be overinterpreted by therapists with allegiance to one or another of them. Yet although all well-structured methods are superior to TAU, none is clearly superior. There should be only one kind of psychotherapy for PD: the one that works. An integrated method would use the best ideas from everyone and put them together into one package (Livesley, 2012).

This conclusion, consistent with research on common factors in all therapies, should be reassuring. Therapists need not be overly concerned that they haven't been trained in the latest method or the latest twist on existing methods. Psychotherapy is placed in a bad light by the endless competition between approaches. In medicine, there is no such thing as a school of treatment specific to any drug; therapeutic agents are used when appropriate and when they complement other interventions. Even so, treatment of BPD cannot be generic but needs to be more specific. For some clinical problems, such as severe substance abuse (W. R. Miller & Rollnick, 2013), new and different methods have been developed. Several of the therapies developed for BPD offer unique interventions that go beyond what clinicians do for most of their patients.

Linehan unlocked a crucial door by placing emphasis on skills for emotion regulation. BPD patients do not recognize their emotions or know how to deal with them, nor do they know how to self-soothe when experiencing difficult feelings. They often do not even know they have had an emotion and move directly to impulsive actions to get rid of a bad or uncomfortable feeling. That is why reviewing the sequence of events before a cut or an overdose is so crucial. Also, even though mindfulness is a difficult technique for most people to learn, even the simplest forms of self-observation can be useful. STEPPS offers a practical method, with down-to-earth pictograms of boiling pots to help people rate the intensity of their emotions. MBT also teaches people to recognize what they feel, but adds an emphasis on the need to recognize what other people are feeling.

Radical acceptance is another important element that is common to all effective therapies. Patients are not encouraged to feel like victims but to come to terms with the past. Most will have had difficult childhoods with adverse events of various kinds. Yet they need to accept the hand that life has dealt them and to accept themselves with all their flaws. Radical acceptance is similar to the famous motto of Alcoholics Anonymous, which advises people to accept what they cannot change.

Rather like the proverbial tale of the blind men and the elephant, each of the specific methods developed to treat these patients looks at the problem of BPD from a different angle, and all have some degree of validity. One can combine the management of emotion dysregulation emphasized by DBT, the ability to observe feelings emphasized by MBT, and the focus on negative thought patterns that characterizes SFT, together with a limited level of exploration and understanding of life histories. These tools are all part of a broad therapeutic armamentarium, nested in an empathic and practical approach, aimed at maximizing the common factors that produce success.

APPLYING EVIDENCE-BASED PRACTICE TO PD TREATMENT AS A WHOLE

When specific methods are developed for the other PDs, they will probably follow many of the same principles described for BPD. What is needed is to define trait domains that can be modified by psychological interventions and to develop interventions that can be used to increase interpersonal skills and reduce negative patterns of behavior. For example, a treatment package that had an effective way of modifying grandiosity could open the door to effective treatment of narcissistic PD. Similarly, a package modifying perfectionism would be the key to treating obsessive–compulsive PD. It is known that CBT programs for treating social anxiety have some effect on avoidant PD (Ahmed et al., 2012), but they have not been extensively tested.

In many ways, psychotherapy for PDs is just beginning. BPD, because of its great clinical burden, will continue to take precedence. However, other PDs, common in clinical and community settings, need specific interventions of their own. Inspired by the success of treatment for BPD, such programs are bound to be developed in the coming decades.

11

Management

In this chapter I must, of necessity, depart to some extent from the evidence-based perspective of this book. The reason is that practitioners have to make decisions about the details of everyday clinical practice that have not been examined in research. Also, although psychotherapies as a complete package have been tested in clinical trials, they are a mixed bag. Most probably, some interventions are highly therapeutic, and others are merely idiosyncratic. Clinicians who want to adopt an eclectic approach need not follow any procedure with absolute fidelity.

I am not proposing a comprehensive treatment model of my own, nor do I want to develop one. However, although an integrated therapy would eventually need its own clinical trials, it can at least be consistent with available evidence. I want to apply common principles derived from the literature, combining the best ideas from many sources. I must acknowledge that like other specialists in personality disorder (PD) treatment,

http://dx.doi.org/10.1037/14642-012
A Concise Guide to Personality Disorders, by J. Paris
Copyright © 2015 by the American Psychological Association. All rights reserved.

some aspects of my approach to management are based on my experience (as well as the experience of working in a clinical team).

This chapter examines some of the problems that trouble therapists of patients with PD and make management difficult and considers principles that could be used to minimize them. The first focus is the tendency of patients to resist change and be in interminable treatment. The second is the frightening chronic suicidality that therapists need to manage in patients with BPD.

PSYCHOTHERAPY: TERMINABLE AND INTERMINABLE

Patients with PDs are often lonely. This leads them to become overly attached, either to therapists or to the mental health system. They need to understand that recovery requires finding a place in the community and a social role. Otherwise, therapy becomes not a means to an end but an end in itself. Goals for change need to be set and agreed on and used to monitor progress. If rehabilitation is not a patient's goal, then there is no point in undertaking treatment.

Patients with PD are known to be at risk for interminable therapy. This problem arises because their lives are unsatisfying, making them anxiously attached to their therapists, and using the protected treatment setting to compensate for deficient social networks. Patients with borderline PD (BPD) sometimes see the mental health system as a setting where they cannot be rejected. Patients with narcissistic PD, who believe they are interesting, may enjoy treatment but fail to commit themselves to change; in common parlance, they talk the talk, but don't walk the walk. Patients with avoidant PD, who only feel safe with people they know well, may not translate what they learn in therapy to an interpersonal context. Patients with compulsive PD, who maintain emotional control through intellectualization, are better at theorizing than at putting ideas into practice.

Interminability is a problem for all forms of talking therapy, but practitioners need to be aware how personality traits can stand in the way of effective therapy. This is why we need to make every session count and avoid drift or stalemate. Every therapy must also include, from the first sessions, a plan for termination.

In any treatment, there will always be work left undone, but therapy that goes on too long becomes counterproductive. This problem was first recognized and described by Freud (1937/1962). What the founder of psychoanalysis did not understand, however, is that patients who are lonely and fulfilled may be reluctant to "graduate" from therapy. Most eventually get past this obstacle, and it is possible to make the termination phase of treatment a productive experience. Yet unfortunately, the "Woody Allen scenario" of endless therapy is not unusual, at least in patients who are either rich or have generous insurance coverage. I have seen quite a few "lifers," as one researcher for the Menninger study of long-term psychotherapy (L. Horwitz, 1974) called such patients.

The best way to get around the problem is never to offer open-ended therapy. All psychotherapies need a contract with a time frame, and careful review must take place before renewing that contract. This focuses the mind of both participants and encourages active collaboration for change. It also protects patients from wasting their time and therapists from feeling trapped into keeping patients until they move away or die.

Another option is to provide intermittent rather than continuous courses of treatment. This idea, first proposed 70 years ago by Alexander and French (1946), is designed to work against the tendency of open-ended therapy to be addictive. It also leaves the door open for "retreads" when circumstances require another course of treatment (Paris, 2007b). It is best to assume that almost all periods of therapy for PD will be brief.

Why, then, do so many mental health practitioners believe that patients with PD need long-term therapy? The main reason is that the problems associated with these conditions are so severe, it seems impossible to treat patients in a few months. Yet there is little empirical evidence that a long course of illness necessarily requires a long course of treatment. In most cases, even in the more severe PDs, there will have been periods of successful functioning on which treatment can build. Even when this is not the case, empirical data fail to support therapy that goes on for years. In contrast, a large body of evidence shows that shorter interventions can be effective for a wide range of psychopathology (Crits-Christoph, Gibbons, & Mukherjee, 2013). Therapist time is a scarce resource that should never be wasted.

Psychotherapists need realistic goals. If they are out to "cure" a PD, they will feel impelled to invest much time in each patient, but if they are realistic and accept that a significant reduction in symptoms is a good enough result, they will treat more people and be more effective with all of them. Therapy can stop when patients' own healing mechanisms begin to kick in and when they have learned enough from treatment to continue the recovery process on their own. This principle is consistent with the idea that patients need to develop a sense of agency in their own lives and not to depend on therapists to do everything for them. Similarly, therapists need to be comfortable with the idea that life is a journey and that patients can be discharged without being "cured."

THREE BASIC PRINCIPLES FOR MANAGEMENT

1. Making a Contract

All therapies require a mutually agreed contract. One should not embark on an expensive, demanding, and time-consuming venture without defining goals and setting a time frame. Like a business plan, a therapy contract encourages focus and reduces drift.

2. Learning New Skills

Much of the work in psychotherapy consists of reassessing problematic behaviors and suggesting alternatives that work better. Instead of detailed exploration of the past, or blanket support, treatment needs a large component of psychoeducation. Teaching skills usually involves unlearning dysfunctional behaviors, and learning more effective interpersonal strategies. As discussed in the previous chapter, Marsha Linehan (1993) pioneered this skill-based approach. These ideas are designed for the treatment of BPD, but the same methods could help a wider range of patients who are dysregulated and impulsive. Dialectical behavior therapy (DBT) has also been tested for managing substance abuse (Dimeff & Linehan, 2008), a problem often comorbid with BPD and in which emotion dysregulation and impulsivity are also striking. Systems training for emotional predictability and problem solving (Black, Blum, McCormick, & Allen, 2013) and mentalization-based treatment (Allen, Fonagy, & Bateman, 2008), both of which are discussed in Chapter 10, have been tested in forensic populations in which some patients with antisocial PD have similarities to BPD.

3. Getting a Life

This is a key principle for treating PD (Zanarini, 2008). No matter what else is addressed in therapy, patients need something to commit to. Freud, when asked what mental health is, said it consists of love and work, but work almost always needs to come first.

Many patients mistakenly believe that "love is the answer," but you have to be somebody before you can love somebody. You cannot find stable love without having an identity of your own. Searching for love without finding yourself raises impossible expectations and usually ends in disaster. Moreover, investing all your emotional capital in one relationship is risky—it gives you nothing to fall back on.

For this reason, patients who come to treatment after the loss of a relationship can be encouraged to take a break from intimacy until they feel better about themselves, and then consider trying again. Although not everyone takes this advice, many will. It is much more important to develop a social role and a social network. Thus, every patient should be encouraged to work, or to go to school to prepare for work. Moreover, to recover, patients need *social capital*, that is, friends and a community (Paris, 2014b).

For these reasons, putting patients with PDs on disability is poison for therapy. Certifying patients for long-term benefits gives up any possibility of rehabilitation. When you sign, you are agreeing that your patient will never be able to work. It can be argued that this can sometimes be true. Yet even the most disabled patients can be asked to volunteer as a way to determine if they have that potential.

A STEPPED CARE MODEL FOR
THE TREATMENT OF BPD

My rationale for treating patients briefly is based on the principle of *stepped care* (Paris, 2013b). This is a model of service delivery in which one begins with less intensive and time-limited treatment to see how helpful that can be. Only when that fails should one consider longer and more expensive therapy.

Since 2001, I have been in charge of a clinic that treats patients with BPD within a 12-week time frame. Each patient receives 24 sessions (12 individual and 12 group). We use a combination of group with psychoeducation and individual sessions, which has been found in most studies to be better than either alone. This short-term program is designed for patients with BPD who are more acute and less disabled and therefore able to benefit from a few months of treatment. The content is a kind of "DBT light" with an eclectic admixture.

Our experience is that among the patients who stay with us for 12 weeks, most will make a fair degree of progress. We have pre–post data on 130 patients seen between 2005 and 2007 that documents improvement in most cases (excluding the 30% of patients who dropped out). Scores on a number of standard measures (Symptom Check List—90, Barratt Impulsivity Scale, and Beck Depression Scale) went down significantly after treatment. Although patients might have improved to the same extent without treatment, most had multiple courses of unsuccessful therapy in the past. Further, if it were true that all patients with BPD need long-term therapy, we would not have seen measurable change within a few months.

We used these findings in 2008 when the hospital asked us to justify the value of our programs; however, pre–post data lack a control group, so we have not published these results. For the same reason that reports claiming to show improvement in long-term therapy require comparisons with briefer forms of treatment, improvement in short-term therapy needs to be compared with naturalistic remission. Nonetheless, we found that emergency department visits and hospital admissions (of particular interest to the hospital administration) went down by about half. We were able to convince the hospital to fund us, even if we could not reach firm conclusions.

Follow-up telephone calls made a year later to most patients also tended to document further progress. Although there were continuing difficulties, most continued to apply skills they had been taught and felt they were continuing to learn new ones. Thus, although we cannot be sure how effective we are, we tend to doubt that the patients we treat would have improved just as much with no intervention at all.

Treating patients with PD briefly has attracted some research support. Most of the gains in DBT occur fairly quickly (Stanley, Brodsky, Nelson, & Dulit, 2007), and many patients with BPD do well after 25 sessions (Davidson, Tyrer, Norrie, Palmer, & Tyrer, 2010). We therefore treat most of our BPD patients in the 12-week program, particularly those who are younger and less chronic.

Patients who are more disabled can be referred to a longer program designed for the rehabilitation of chronic patients. We also use this as a backup option in a stepped care model for those who fail to respond to 12 weeks of therapy. The separate clinics for extended care have a time scale up to 18 to 24 months. Although results are necessarily more limited in this highly dysfunctional population, pre–post data suggest that most are less symptomatic after treatment. The difference is that although most patients coming to the brief program are working or attending school, many of those coming to long-term treatment are on welfare or long-term disability. We encourage all patients to get back to work (or go to school), and some of them do. If this is not possible, we can still encourage our patients to get more involved in activities, either in the family or in the community.

The main advantage of a stepped care model is that it allows us to manage a large number of patients. I work in general hospitals where there is a constant inflow of patients with BPD through emergency departments and crisis teams. There is certainly no lack of work to be done. In the absence of specialized but brief programs, these patients tend either to move in and out of the system or to be stuck in it without making progress.

I am interested in reaching out to the community, so I carry out several hundred consultations a year. Once seen, patients who are able to engage in our programs do not have to wait for more than a few weeks for therapy. Most, particularly when younger and more acute, need rapidly accessible interventions. Our program opens up access to patients who would otherwise have to be put on waiting lists for treatment (as happens in other settings offering specialized services). This is not to say that all patients who have been to the emergency department are ready for psychotherapy. They may refuse treatment, fail to come to sessions, or drop out. However, these cases can always be reevaluated at a later time to see whether motivation has become stronger.

A stepped care model allows for intermittent courses of therapy, and patients who come back with serious problems after completing a 12-week program can be offered the longer option. However, if there is no progress after 24 months, we do not offer further treatment because continuing beyond that point is unlikely to be profitable, and we return these patients to community care.

These principles can also be applied to clinical practice outside specialized settings: Most practitioners can apply the stepped care model. It has been established that this is a good way to allocate scarce services in all forms of chronic disease, and the model has been applied to other disorders in medicine and psychiatry that have a variable prognosis (Paris, 2013c). Because prognosis is generally variable, it makes little sense to offer the same treatment to every patient. Many will recover rapidly, and only some become chronically disabled. One cannot know the prognosis at intake, and thus the treatment model moves by steps, with brief therapy as the default condition, reserving resource-heavy interventions for those who fail to recover. The model also allows for intermittent therapy, in which patients are discharged to see how well they make use of the first step. A good rule of thumb is to ask patients to apply what they have learned and to wait 6 months before returning for reassessment.

The discovery that psychotherapy, when properly conducted, helps most people with BPD is one of the most promising developments over my lifetime as a clinician. Younger clinicians may see the same principles applied to all PDs. Yet there will always be patients who do not do well in psychotherapy, or in any other form of treatment. This is a fact we have to live with: "Radical acceptance" is as necessary for us as it is for our clients. It does not make sense to continue to see treatment failures on a regular basis, because that blocks access to new patients who will gain more benefit.

Although there is only a small literature on the brief treatment of PD (Paris, 2007b), Anthony Bateman, who developed mentalization-based treatment, has told me that he now thinks it may be more useful to treat BPD intermittently rather than continuously. This option works against stalemates, while maintaining availability for later consultation or therapy "retreads."

Although we lack treatment protocols for PDs other than BPD, a stepped care approach might also be applicable for patients with other trait profiles and for the mixed picture seen in PD, not otherwise specified. One common element in all disorders is interpersonal and occupational dysfunction that seriously interferes with quality of life. A stepped care model for all these patients would also emphasize rehabilitation and the accumulation of social capital (Paris, 2014b).

Psychotherapy is too dependent on market forces. Paying patients who can afford to come regularly for months or years may be seen as a plus by clinicians. In contrast, providing evidence-based therapy for patients with PD requires a commitment to accessibility. An all-too-common scenario is that specialized treatment is only available to a small minority: those who have money, those whose families have money, and those who are lucky enough to get in before a clinic is forced to put prospective patients on a waiting list.

Where I work (Canada), psychiatric treatment is insured by the government, but most psychiatrists do little psychotherapy. The main portal of entry into the mental health system is the hospital emergency department. Many patients receive a few sessions of follow-up after that or end up in general follow-up, receiving medication instead of treatment from a team well trained in the specific management of their disorder. By and large, PD patients do not do well in standard outpatient follow-up. Stepped care provides an alternative model, allowing for the allocation of scarce but effective resources to these complex clinical problems.

MANAGING SUICIDALITY IN BPD

Chronic suicidality is a hallmark of BPD, and fear of losing a patient to suicide can get in the way of conducting effective treatment. When you are constantly afraid your patients will kill themselves, it is hard to do any useful work. If therapists respond to every suicidal threat as if the patient's life is in danger, treatment comes to a complete standstill.

To treat chronically suicidal patients, clinicians need to understand that the possibility of suicide is part of the territory. Some patients do actually kill themselves, but that is more likely to happen when they are out of treatment. Most of the time, suicidality is a way of coping with pain. Paradoxically, preoccupation with death can itself become a way of life (Paris, 2006).

It follows that clinicians need not overreact to self-harm incidents or to small overdoses that are immediately brought to the attention of significant others. This does not, of course, mean that one should ignore such events. Rather, they need to be understood as ways of expressing distress, albeit dramatically. Instead of a panicky referral to the emergency department, one can conduct a careful inquiry about the source of distress and the sequence of events that led up to the crisis. Sending patients with PD to hospitals has never been shown to have benefit or to prevent suicide. Moreover, hospitalization is often counterproductive because it puts patients in an artificial environment and interferes with life tasks that need to be mastered. It interrupts therapy without accomplishing anything useful; it takes patients away from their problems temporarily but also removes them from the domains in which they are functioning. Hospital wards may offer a breathing space but staying there solves nothing.

Ironically, some patients insist on going to hospital. For most people, the emergency department would be an unpleasant place to spend an evening or to stay overnight. Yet patients whose quality of life is low may prefer this environment to going home. Although most patients in the emergency department agree to leave after being evaluated, some escalate their threats to force staff to keep them. If the cycle continues, patients tend to be fully admitted.

In the United States, managed care has done patients with PD a real favor by refusing to provide coverage for more than a few days of hospital care. However, in the fully insured system in which I work, I have seen patients remain on hospital wards for months when they continue to threaten suicide every time discharge is brought up. When this happens, admission becomes a purely custodial procedure.

Some governments in Europe pay for extended hospital stays for patients with PD, usually in specialized inpatient programs. This is an expensive option that can almost certainly be carried out in other ways. Specialized programs for PD can be better located in day hospitals, as has been shown by Piper, Rosie, and Joyce (1996), as well as by Bateman and Fonagy (2004).

The use of hospitalization for PD is rooted in confusion between the acute suicidality seen in classical mood disorders and the chronic suicidality that characterizes BPD. In the first case, one applies specific methods of treatment that can best be handled on an inpatient unit, where drugs can produce a remission of a temporary state of suicidality. In the second case, patients are admitted but not treated and continue being chronically suicidal once they are discharged. There is no evidence that keeping patients on a hospital ward, even under constant observation, prevents from them from killing themselves in either the short or long term. When suicidality is chronic, death by suicide is a risk that must be accepted (Maltsberger, 1994). In any case, chronically suicidal patients who do commit suicide rarely die in the acute crises that bring them to emergency department. Instead, they are more at risk later in the course of the disorder, when they give up hope after a long series of unsuccessful treatments (Paris, 2003). No therapist wants to lose a patient to suicide, but we do not know how to predict it, even using standard algorithms based on known risk factors (Paris, 2006). In BPD, where some of the risk factors for suicide, such as serious previous attempts and substance abuse (Stone, 1990), are known, statistical relationships do not translate into prediction because these effects are too small to have any useful clinical application.

Understanding chronic suicidality as a form of communication offers a way out of these dilemmas. Patients who threaten and attempt suicide feel unheard and invalidated; but when they talk of death, significant others and mental health professionals will listen. This is not to dismiss suicidality as mere attention seeking. Suicidal ideas need to be taken seriously, but not in the way that one might think—that is, doing something radical to prevent suicide. Instead we need to provide empathy for the suffering that makes patients consider ending their lives.

Thus, one of the most useful responses therapists can make to a suicidal threat is to reflect on how bad the patient must be feeling to consider that option. It is important to validate emotions, even when a therapist feels under pressure. Empathy also makes it easier to move to a problem-solving mode. This can be framed in statements such as, "You can always kill yourself, but let's see if we can come up with alternatives to help you through the crisis you're in now." There are also times when patients accuse a therapist of not caring enough to stop them from committing suicide. The answer has to be, "In the long run, I can't stop you, but I believe we can work together to find another solution."

These responses provide implicit validation of autonomy. Patients can be attached to their suicidality and find it comforting. They are, to borrow a phrase from John Keats, "half in love with death." Their life is more tolerable if they know that, if necessary, they can leave it. For this very reason, therapists need to accept suicidality to treat it.

Therapists are understandably terrified about suicide, but it is a tragic experience that will happen, at least occasionally, to almost any clinician who works with seriously ill people (Chemtob, Hamada, Bauer, Torigoe, & Kinney, 1988). It is part of the landscape of psychotherapy. Because no one knows how to predict suicide, clinicians working in this context must live with the risk. The only effective ways of preventing suicide that have been supported by research are population-based interventions that make it more difficult to access the means to kill oneself (Paris, 2006).

In our litigious society, therapists are also afraid of being sued by families if their patients die by suicide. Although this possibility cannot be ruled out, there are ways to make such an outcome less likely (Gutheil, 2004). The first is to keep careful notes, explaining in detail why one is intervening (or not intervening). A second is to obtain consultation from a trusted colleague. The third, and most important, is to bring families into therapy at an early point to explain the risk of suicide and gain their cooperation in a plan that aims to treat the patient rather than consign him or her to a cycle of repeated admissions.

Chronic suicidality is wearing for therapists, some of whom try to avoid taking on patients who appear to be at high risk. Yet patients who improve sufficiently to discard the option of suicide can be one of the most validating experiences in the practice of psychotherapy.

In summary, constantly worrying about suicide reinforces pathology by putting the therapist in the position of an anxious caretaker who is responsible for the patient's welfare (just the sort of relationship that chronically suicidal patients tend to have on the outside). In contrast, empathizing with the suffering that makes people want to leave the world is helpful and avoids agreeing with suicidal patients that feelings can be replaced with actions.

CLINICAL EXAMPLES

I now provide illustrations of how some of the principles described in this chapter can be applied to patients with PD. I have drawn all these examples, which have varying outcomes, from our 12-week program for BPD.

Patients Who Made Significant Progress

Arlene was a 22-year-old woman referred following a severe overdose, after which she made further suicidal threats. The precipitant was a breakup with a boyfriend, part of a long-term pattern of infatuation with unsuitable men. She was, however, able to be competent and stable in her work as a secretary.

In individual therapy, Arlene came to understand that her problems associated with feeling rejected by men were related to an absent father. Her biological father had moved to another city when she was a child and forgot about her. But Arlene was also in chronic conflict with her mother and had a difficult relationship to her stepfather. In group therapy, she was taught a number of skills that follow the principles of DBT and are part of our treatment module: emotion regulation, appropriate assertiveness, and thinking before acting out impulsively.

Arlene made a change by moving out of the house. She also realized she needed a break before becoming involved with another boyfriend and developed a social network with other women. At 1-year follow-up, she had returned to school and was no longer contemplating suicide.

Shirley was a 25-year-old nurse. Symptoms included cutting, suicidal ideas, and chronic depression with insomnia. She was living with her mother and stepfather. Her relationships to men were impulsive and unstable. In individual therapy, Shirley described a problematic relationship with her father, a physician who was both inconsistent and rejecting, much like her boyfriends. In group therapy, she was taught how to manage her emotions to avoid cutting and was able to find better ways of soothing herself, primarily through increasing the number of female friends in her life. On 2-year follow-up, Shirley had a good job and had found a much more supportive man. Although she continued to have periods of low mood, she no longer carried out self-destructive actions.

Norma was a 24-year-old student who grew up in an Inuit community in the Arctic. She was referred for cutting, suicidality, unstable relations, and olfactory hallucinations (i.e., she thought she had a bad smell). Symptomatic change was associated with finding a stable social network, partly through the Inuit community in the city, where she found role models, and partly from the women she met at school. Norma stopped cutting, and decided to take a break from men. On 1-year follow-up, she maintained these gains and planned a career in social services.

Patients Who Improved Up to a Point

Maureen was a 24-year-old farmworker referred for suicidality, cutting, and chronic depression. Eighteen months earlier, Maureen had gone through a divorce, followed by a series of unsatisfying relationships with men, finally moving back with her parents. She was only able to work part time on a dairy farm.

Maureen was motivated enough to do a 2-hour drive to come to the city for treatment. In individual therapy, one key issue was a history of sexual abuse by a cousin that lasted over 4 years. This had occurred because of emotional isolation within the family, in which she felt entirely misunderstood, but she also felt scarred and stigmatized.

In group therapy, Maureen was encouraged to overcome her difficulty in being intimate and trusting and to overcome the feeling that no one could ever find her special. Maureen was somewhat improved after therapy: She was able to keep her job and stopped seeing an uncommitted boyfriend. On 6-month follow-up, however, she felt lonely and pessimistic about stable intimacy.

Maria was a 26-year-old woman living alone on welfare, having recently dropped out of university. Her symptoms include cutting, suicidal threats, substance abuse, and chronic shoplifting (for which she faced a court date). After her parents divorced, her mother was murdered by a lover. Maria had also been involved with abusive men, and although she currently had a supportive boyfriend, she was not faithful to him.

Maria attended the program regularly and at discharge was less impulsive, particularly in relation to alcohol intake. On 6-month follow-up, she had made plans to go to school to learn how to be a hairdresser. However, it was not clear that she would be able to establish a stable intimate relationship.

Patients Who Failed to Respond to Treatment

Jean was a 25-year-old woman referred to our PD program for chronic suicidality. Jean has not been able to make any commitments in life and became heavily involved in drinking and drugs. She broke up with a boyfriend and grieved for him, although they had spent most of their time together taking cocaine. Jean came from a middle-class family but rejected "conventional" values without being able to come up with an alternative or a direction.

Jean regarded treatment with ironic detachment, not getting emotionally involved. Although she was able to moderate her substance abuse, she did not seriously look for work and continued to depend on her parents financially.

Karen was a 42-year-old unemployed woman who was referred after an overdose. The crisis was associated with the loss of a boyfriend who moved away to another city. Karen had little life of her own and never had. She had long been involved with substance abuse, and her only work history was as an escort. Karen did not feel a strong need for treatment and dropped out of our program after a few weeks.

Although the results of a program such as ours are inevitably variable, our team is satisfied to be able to help a good percentage of those who enter it. We know that not every patient with a PD is treatable at any given time and that this is a difficult population, so we accept limitations. Good responses to brief treatment are gratifying if therapists keep expectations reasonable and value small victories. By and large, those who do best are those who have shown previous strengths in work and in relationships. Motivation for change and persistence, however difficult to measure or predict, may also determine outcome.

Most patients in research studies have been documented to show symptomatic improvement, but we are skeptical of claims of personality change, usually based on a few highly successful cases. Rather, we aim to help patients find a way to make their personality work better. To be emotionally labile is not necessarily a bad thing, particularly when one no longer responds to one's sensitivity by cutting, overdosing, or using substances.

A PHILOSOPHY OF MANAGEMENT

The management of PD need not be an exercise in perfectionism. Many patients go into remission and may even offer therapists heartwarming gratitude. Those who make a partial recovery should still be counted as successes. I am trained in medicine, in which most pathology is chronic and cures are exceptional. As for cases who fail to respond to reasonable efforts at treatment, there is no point banging our heads against walls. (As some of our patients do.)

This is the philosophy that makes me happy to treat difficult patients. I want challenging work that requires the skills I have learned over several decades, but I do not want to trap myself in unreasonable expectations. My hope is that the readers of this book will give up looking for absolute answers and accept that if they can help most of the people they see, they are doing well.

12

Summary and Future Directions

WHERE WE HAVE COME FROM AND WHERE WE ARE NOW

The concept of a personality disorder (PD) is relatively recent but is consistent with theoretical and empirical work in psychology. The construct emerged from psychoanalytic theories about the structure of the mind but is independent of that model, now rooted in trait psychology. The principle that both personality and PD arise from gene–environment interactions has been confirmed by behavior genetics, and outcome research has shown that these diagnoses are stable. Finally, the concept of PD is consistent with cognitive neuroscience and with research on emotion regulation.

Although much still needs to be learned about the causes of PDs, what we know generally fits into a biopsychosocial model. Thus, biological temperament, life experiences, and the social environment all play

http://dx.doi.org/10.1037/14642-013
A Concise Guide to Personality Disorders, by J. Paris

a role in etiology. Research has to take all of these factors into account. It also requires a better understanding of the relations among heritable temperament, the development of stable traits, and the risk for PD. This line of research requires longitudinal data. For example, one of the more important recent findings is that temperament can produce *differential susceptibility* to the environment, so that some personality characteristics can lead to either disorder or to better functioning, depending on what happens to people over the course of their lives (Belsky & Pluess, 2009). These findings confirm the view, best developed by Beck and Freeman (2002), that our personality can either work for us or against us, depending on circumstance.

The other recent development that has led to controversy about PD concerns the *Diagnostic and Statistical Manual of Mental Disorders* (5th ed.; *DSM–5;* American Psychiatric Association, 2013). Although the current classification of PDs leaves a great deal to be desired, it is neither better nor worse than the systems we use to classify other major mental disorders. I have a larger concern. Clinicians have not yet embraced the complexity of personality and PD. Too often they prefer the simplicity of symptoms seen as a clearer focus for treatment.

The greatest progress in PD research in recent decades has concerned outcome and treatment. The idea that PDs are incurable can now be firmly rejected. It was based almost entirely on the "clinician's illusion," in which illness is seen as more chronic than it really is. Careful follow-up of patients with a range of PDs shows that most improve with time. This finding could reduce the stigma of PD in which perceptions of hopelessness have interfered with the recognition of these conditions. This is not to say that patients with PDs do not continue to have problems—most of them do— but we all have problematic traits, and most of us manage to live productive lives in spite of them.

Research showing that borderline PD (BPD) can be successfully treated was a dramatic breakthrough for the field. Most of the credit belongs to Marsha Linehan, who rethought the problem from scratch and came up with creative and highly effective solutions. Others have developed parallel or similar methods, and we now understand the basic principles of therapy for this population. Of equal importance, ineffective methods of therapy that dominated the field for too long are being gradually discarded.

FUTURE DIRECTIONS AND UNANSWERED QUESTIONS

Further progress in research on PD is not predictable, but new paradigms could emerge to change the field. Our knowledge could be further extended by following some of the most promising current developments.

Childhood Precursors and Prevention

Research on the childhood precursors of PD has been developing rapidly, focusing largely on BPD. The etiological pathways that drive personality pathology should be further illuminated by longitudinal studies of populations at risk, whether that risk is due to abnormal temperament or to psychosocial adversity. Although it may never be possible to write an equation or a formula for "cooking" a PD, we could be in a position to define which children are most likely to develop one.

Doing so would allow us to consider methods of prevention and early intervention. For example, early psychoeducational interventions in schools and in the home have been shown to reduce drug use among adolescents at risk (Castellanos-Ryan, Séguin, Vitaro, Parent, & Tremblay, 2013). If addictions, a problem as stubborn as PD (and highly comorbid with PD), can be at least partially prevented, then the same might be accomplished for symptoms of antisocial PD and BPD.

Adolescent Onset

Because we now know that PD begins early in life and because it may have a higher prevalence in adolescence that it does later, it makes little sense to wait until patients are 18 years old to diagnose it. Although adolescents are difficult to engage in therapy, it has been shown that at least some of them can benefit from early interventions, particularly when they are well thought out and systematic.

Because not everyone examines the manual closely, here is what *DSM–5* has to say:

> For a personality disorder to be diagnosed in an individual younger than 18 years, the features must have been present for at least 1 year. The one exception to this is antisocial personality disorder, which cannot be diagnosed in individuals younger than 18 years. (American Psychiatric Association, 2013, pp. 247–248)

We have an important job to do in convincing clinicians not to dismiss PD as a "phase" that adolescents can be expected to grow out of. Although that sometimes happens, most of these patients continue to have serious problems in adulthood and require both accurate diagnosis and evidence-based treatment.

Community Prevalence

Over the past few decades, epidemiological research has taken PD seriously. If the word can get out that antisocial PD affects 2% to 3% of the population and that BPD can be found in almost 1%, this will increase clinical awareness. The main problem is that all these estimates are based on dicey criteria derived from the *DSM* system. We also need to be careful about overestimates of community prevalence, which could be used to discredit rather than to support PD diagnoses.

Clinical Prevalence

One of the most ironic aspects of current practice is that although PDs are common, they often go unrecognized. We need to develop simpler and more user-friendly ways of assessing PDs. It may be even more important to teach clinicians that they ignore them at their peril and that patients suffer if life histories are not taken and long-term psychopathology is not properly considered.

Biological Research

It is difficult to treat PDs if we do not understand them. To solve these problems, much hope has been placed on neuroscience. We now know much more about how the brain functions. Unfortunately, despite the billions of research dollars spent on biological research in the past 20 years, it has told us little of direct relevance to the treatment of mental illness. The investment may pan out eventually, but there are good reasons to be cautious. The clinical phenomena that characterize PD lie at a level of complexity that will be difficult to correlate with changes in brain structure of functioning as measured by imaging. We need more basic knowledge to come up with hypotheses that are specific to any disorder. In the meantime, more needs to be done to study key variables such as affective instability.

Gene–Environment Interactions

The phenomena that characterize PDs are difficult to correlate with genes or with changes in the epigenome. Yet not enough research has been conducted on the gene–environment interactions that drive psychopathology. The obstacles are that genetic knowledge is still fairly primitive and we lack sophisticated and accurate ways of measuring environmental factors. Simplistic approaches, in which genetic variants are linked to broad developmental risk such as "abuse," have failed to address this problem. Further, because an outcome of PD is marked by equifinality, we will need large samples to sort out the interactions that raise risk for serious psychopathology.

Making Treatment Accessible

Current treatments of PD, even when evidence based, have a long way to go to become accessible. The best studied method, dialectical behavioral therapy, is expensive and can potentially go on for years, much like psychoanalysis. If it has not been tested for more than 1 year, then it should be offered for only 1 year. Briefer interventions, along the lines of systems training for emotional predictability and problem solving, need to be further developed. Putting patients on waiting lists or requiring them to be wealthy is no way to apply the progress that has been made in treating BPD.

There are few things as inexpensive as prescribing a drug. This is one of the reasons for the decline of psychotherapy as a whole. If we want practitioners to treat PDs, we need to develop methods that help patients within a reasonable time. If there is flow in the system, more patients will be able to enter it.

Extending Treatment Research to Other PDs

It is understandable that research on treatment has focused on BPD, but many of the same principles could be applied to other disorders. What we need are treatment packages specifically designed for the specific problems that each category of disorder presents. One prime candidate for this development is narcissistic PD.

Developing a Better Classification

I have left this issue almost for last. Some researchers want to start with a new system and see where it leads. I would argue that it could be a waste of time to tinker with classification until we know much more. When physicians of the past studied swelling and pain, they made little progress; it was only when they understood the mechanisms behind disease that they could begin to classify it scientifically. Until we can begin to answer such questions, attempts to develop a new diagnostic system may be futile.

Raising Awareness and Recognition

The most urgent need for PD researchers and clinicians who treat these conditions is to raise public awareness of the problem. There is no drug to treat these patients, and thus the pharmaceutical industry is not interested in helping with this agenda. Psychotherapy is the most effective form of treatment for PD. Yet as long as treatment can only be carried out in specialized settings, caregivers, patients, or families may not see it as relevant. These are all reachable goals, and we can expect slow but steady progress in the coming decades. Our patients depend on us to do so.

FOUR MYTHS (AND REALITIES) ABOUT PD

Myth 1: Personality Cannot Change.

Reality: Although personality traits are relatively stable over time, they do show gradual change, mostly for the better. With time, most impulsive people learn to control themselves, anxious people gradually expose themselves to what they fear, and compulsive people learn to give up some degree of control. This is not to say that these trends are universal or that there is no such thing as PD in old age; of course there is. By and large, however, people change for the better as they grow old. Life's greatest distresses occur in the young and the middle-aged, and old age can temper the fires of youth with acceptance and serenity.

Myth 2: PDs Are Not Mental Illnesses.

Reality: The suffering associated with personality pathology is as severe as in other major mental disorders. There is a tendency to dismiss the problem, or redefine it as due to more familiar constructs such as depression or anxiety. We do this only because we are not always familiar with the specific approaches that can work for these patients.

Myth 3: Personality Disorders Are Incurable.

Reality: As we have seen, most people with PD improve gradually, albeit with some degree of residual dysfunction. The idea that PD does not get better is due to the clinician's illusion in which recovered patients stop coming for help, whereas unrecovered patients keep asking for help.

Myth 4: Patients With PDs Cannot Improve in Brief Therapy.

Reality: This belief has led to lengthy, expensive, ineffective, and frustrating therapies. The best becomes the enemy of the good. If you are a seasoned clinician, you will probably have learned to accept small victories, to not try for ideal outcomes, and to be satisfied with helping people to function in life.

The realities listed here are fundamental to a philosophy of treatment for PD. We will learn how to help patients more effectively in the future, but we already know enough to take on difficult cases and to make a real difference.

References

Achenbach, T. M., & Ndetei, D. M. (2012). Clinical models for child and adolescent behavioral, emotional, and social problems. In J. M. Rey (Ed.), *IACAPAP e-textbook of child and adolescent mental health* (pp. 1–30). Geneva, Switzerland: International Association for Child and Adolescent Psychiatry and Allied Professions.

Ahmed, U., Gibbon, S., Jones, H., Huband, N., Ferriter, M., Völlm, B. A., . . . Duggan, C. (2012). Psychological interventions for avoidant personality disorder (protocol). *Cochrane Database of Systematic Reviews, 1*, CD009549. Advance online publication. http://dx.doi.org/10.1002/14651858.CD009549

Akiskal, H. S. (2004). Demystifying borderline personality: Critique of the concept and unorthodox reflections on its natural kinship with the bipolar spectrum. *Acta Psychiatrica Scandinavica, 110*, 401–407. http://dx.doi.org/10.1111/j.1600-0447.2004.00461.x

Akiskal, H. S., Chen, S. E., Davis, G. C., Puzantian, V. R., Kashgarian, M., & Bolinger, J. M. (1985). Borderline: An adjective in search of a noun. *Journal of Clinical Psychiatry, 46*, 41–48.

Alexander, F., & French, T. (1946). *Psychoanalytic therapy.* New York, NY: Ronald Press.

Allen, J. G., Fonagy, P., & Bateman, A. W. (2008). *Mentalizing in clinical practice.* Arlington, VA: American Psychiatric Publishing.

American Psychiatric Association. (1952). *Diagnostic and statistical manual of mental disorders.* Washington, DC: Author.

American Psychiatric Association. (1968). *Diagnostic and statistical manual of mental disorders* (2nd ed.). Washington, DC: Author.

American Psychiatric Association. (1980). *Diagnostic and statistical manual of mental disorders* (3rd ed.). Washington, DC: Author.

American Psychiatric Association. (1994). *Diagnostic and statistical manual of mental disorders* (4th ed.). Washington, DC: Author.

American Psychiatric Association. (2001). Practice guideline for the treatment of borderline personality disorder. *The American Journal of Psychiatry, 158*(Suppl. 10), 1–52.

American Psychiatric Association. (2013). *Diagnostic and statistical manual of mental disorders* (5th ed.). Washington, DC: Author.

Bagby, R. M., Costa, P. T., Jr., Widiger, T. A., Ryder, A. G., & Marshall, M. (2005). DSM–IV personality disorders and the five-factor model of personality: A multi-method examination of domain-and facet-level predictions. *European Journal of Personality, 19*, 307–324. http://dx.doi.org/10.1002/per.563

Baldwin, S. A., & Imel, Z. E. (2013). Therapist effects: Findings and methods. In M. Lambert (Ed.), *Handbook of psychotherapy and behavior change* (pp. 258–297). New York, NY: Wiley.

Bamelis, L. L. M., Evers, S. M. A. A., Spinhoven, P., & Arntz, A. (2014). Results of a multicenter randomized controlled trial of the clinical effectiveness of schema therapy for borderline personality disorder. *The American Journal of Psychiatry, 171*, 305–322. http://dx.doi.org/10.1176/appi.ajp.2013.12040518

Bateman, A., & Fonagy, P. (2001). Treatment of borderline personality disorder with psychoanalytically oriented partial hospitalization: An 18-month follow-up. *The American Journal of Psychiatry, 158*, 36–42. http://dx.doi.org/10.1176/appi.ajp.158.1.36

Bateman, A., & Fonagy, P. (2004). *Psychotherapy for borderline personality disorder: Mentalization-based treatment.* New York, NY: Oxford University Press.

Bateman, A., & Fonagy, P. (2006). *Mentalization-based treatment: A practical guide.* New York, NY: Wiley. http://dx.doi.org/10.1093/med/9780198570905.001.0001

Bateman, A., & Fonagy, P. (2008). 8-year follow-up of patients treated for borderline personality disorder: Mentalization-based treatment versus treatment as usual. *The American Journal of Psychiatry, 165*, 631–638. http://dx.doi.org/10.1176/appi.ajp.2007.07040636

Bateman, A., & Fonagy, P. (2009). Randomized controlled trial of outpatient mentalization-based treatment versus structured clinical management for borderline personality disorder. *The American Journal of Psychiatry, 166*, 1355–1364. http://dx.doi.org/10.1176/appi.ajp.2009.09040539

Batstra, L., & Frances, A. (2012). DSM–5 further inflates attention deficit hyperactivity disorder. *Journal of Nervous and Mental Disease, 200*, 486–488. http://dx.doi.org/10.1097/NMD.0b013e318257c4b6

Beauchaine, T. P., Klein, D. N., Crowell, S. E., Derbidge, C., & Gatzke-Kopp, L. (2009). Multifinality in the development of personality disorders: A Biology × Sex × Environment interaction model of antisocial and borderline traits.

Development and Psychopathology, 21, 735–770. http://dx.doi.org/10.1017/S0954579409000418

Beck, A. T., & Freeman, A. (2002). *Cognitive therapy of personality disorders* (2nd ed.). New York, NY: Guilford Press.

Beck, A. T., & Haigh, E. A. (2014). Advances in cognitive theory and therapy: The generic cognitive model. *Annual Review of Clinical Psychology, 10*, 1–24. http://dx.doi.org/10.1146/annurev-clinpsy-032813-153734

Bedhiran, T., & Sartorius, N. (1995). *Mental illness in general health care: An international study.* New York, NY: Wiley.

Belsky, D. W., Caspi, A., Arseneault, L., Bleidorn, W., Fonagy, P., Goodman, M., . . . Moffitt, T. E. (2012). Etiological features of borderline personality related characteristics in a birth cohort of 12-year-old children. *Development and Psychopathology, 24*, 251–265. http://dx.doi.org/10.1017/S0954579411000812

Belsky, J., & Pluess, M. (2009). The nature (and nurture?) of plasticity in early human development. *Perspectives on Psychological Science, 4*, 345–351. http://dx.doi.org/10.1111/j.1745-6924.2009.01136.x

Belsky, J., & Pluess, M. (2013). Genetic moderation of early child-care effects on social functioning across childhood: A developmental analysis. *Child Development, 84*, 1209–1225. http://dx.doi.org/10.1111/cdev.12058

Berg-Nielsen, T. S., Vikan, A., & Dahl, A. A. (2002). Parenting related to child and parental psychopathology: A descriptive review of the literature. *Clinical Child Psychology and Psychiatry, 7*, 529–552. http://dx.doi.org/10.1177/1359104502007004006

Berrios, G. E. (1993). European views on personality disorders: A conceptual history. *Comprehensive Psychiatry, 34*, 14–30. http://dx.doi.org/10.1016/0010-440X(93)90031-X

Biskin, R. S., Paris, J., Renaud, J., Raz, A., & Zelkowitz, P. (2011). Outcomes in women diagnosed with borderline personality disorder in adolescence. *Journal of the Canadian Academy of Child and Adolescent Psychiatry, 20*, 168–174.

Black, D. W. (2013a). *Bad boys, bad men* (2nd ed.). New York, NY: Oxford University Press.

Black, D. W. (2013b). *DSM–5* is approved, but personality disorders criteria have not changed. *Annals of Clinical Psychiatry, 25*, 1.

Black, D. W., Baumgard, C. H., & Bell, S. E. (1995). A 16- to 45-year follow-up of 71 men with antisocial personality disorder. *Comprehensive Psychiatry, 36*, 130–140. http://dx.doi.org/10.1016/S0010-440X(95)90108-6

Black, D. W., Blum, N., McCormick, B., & Allen, J. (2013). Systems Training for Emotional Predictability and Problem Solving (STEPPS) group treatment for offenders with borderline personality disorder. *Journal of Nervous and Mental Disease, 201*, 124–129. http://dx.doi.org/10.1097/NMD.0b013e31827f6435

Black, D. W., Gunter, T., Loveless, P., Allen, J., & Sieleni, B. (2010). Antisocial personality disorder in incarcerated offenders: Psychiatric comorbidity and quality of life. *Annals of Clinical Psychiatry, 22,* 113–120.

Black, D. W., Zanarini, M. C., Romine, A., Shawn, M., Allen, J., & Schulz, S. C. (2014). Comparison of low and moderate dosages of extended-release quetiapine in borderline personality disorder: A randomized, double-blind, placebo-controlled trial. *The American Journal of Psychiatry.* Advance online publication. http://dx.doi.org/10.1176/appi.ajp.2014.13101348

Bloom, P. (2013). *Just babies: The origins of good and evil.* New York, NY: Crown.

Blum, N., St. John, D., Pfohl, B., Stuart, S., McCormick, B., Allen, J., . . . Black, D. W. (2008). Systems training for emotional predictability and problem solving (STEPPS) for outpatients with borderline personality disorder: A randomized controlled trial and 1-year follow-up. *The American Journal of Psychiatry, 165,* 468–478. http://dx.doi.org/10.1176/appi.ajp.2007.07071079

Bohart, A. C., & Greaves-Wade, A. (2013). The client in psychotherapy. In M. Lambert (Ed.), *Handbook of psychotherapy and behavior change* (pp. 219–257). New York, NY: Wiley.

Bornovalova, M., Huibregste, B. M., & Hicks, B. M. (2013). Tests of a direct effect of childhood abuse on adult borderline personality disorder traits: A longitudinal discordant twin design. *Journal of Abnormal Psychology, 122,* 180–194. http://dx.doi.org/10.1037/a0028328

Bornstein, R. F. (2005). *The dependent patient: A practitioner's guide.* Washington, DC: American Psychological Association. http://dx.doi.org/10.1037/11085-000

Bos, E. H., van der Wel, E. B., Appelo, M. T., & Verbraak, M. J. (2010). A randomized controlled trial of a Dutch version of systems training for emotional predictability and problem solving for borderline personality disorder. *Journal of Nervous and Mental Disease, 198,* 299–304. http://dx.doi.org/10.1097/NMD.0b013e3181d619cf

Brown, M. Z., Comtois, K. A., & Linehan, M. M. (2002). Reasons for suicide attempts and nonsuicidal self-injury in women with borderline personality disorder. *Journal of Abnormal Psychology, 111,* 198–202. http://dx.doi.org/10.1037/0021-843X.111.1.198

Cain, N. M., Pincus, A. L., & Ansell, E. B. (2008). Narcissism at the crossroads: Phenotypic description of pathological narcissism across clinical theory, social/personality psychology, and psychiatric diagnosis. *Clinical Psychology Review, 28,* 638–656. http://dx.doi.org/10.1016/j.cpr.2007.09.006

Campbell, W. K., & Miller, J. D. (Eds.). (2011). *Handbook of narcissism and narcissistic personality disorder.* New York, NY: Wiley. http://dx.doi.org/10.1002/9781118093108

Carver, C. S., & Miller, C. J. (2006). Relations of serotonin function to personality: Current views and a key methodological issue. *Psychiatry Research*, *144*, 1–15.

Caspi, A., McClay, J., Moffitt, T. E., Mill, J., Martin, J., & Craig, I.W., . . . Poulton, R. (2002). Role of genotype in the cycle of violence in maltreated children. *Science*, *297*, 851–854. http://dx.doi.org/10.1126/science.1072290

Caspi, A., Moffitt, T. E., Newman, D. L., & Silva, P. A. (1996). Behavioral observations at age 3 years predict adult psychiatric disorders. Longitudinal evidence from a birth cohort. *Archives of General Psychiatry*, *53*, 1033–1039. http://dx.doi.org/10.1001/archpsyc.1996.01830110071009

Caspi, A., & Roberts, B. W. (1999). Personality change and continuity across the lifetime. In L. A. Pervin & O. P. John (Eds.), *Handbook of personality: Theory and research* (2nd ed., pp. 300–326). New York, NY: Guilford Press.

Castellanos-Ryan, N., Séguin, J. R., Vitaro, F., Parent, S., & Tremblay, R. E. (2013). Impact of a 2-year multimodal intervention for disruptive 6-year-olds on substance use in adolescence: Randomised controlled trial. *The British Journal of Psychiatry*, *203*, 188–195. http://dx.doi.org/10.1192/bjp.bp.112.123182

Chanen, A. M., & McCutcheon, L. (2013). Prevention and early intervention for borderline personality disorder: Current status and recent evidence. *The British Journal of Psychiatry Supplement*, *54*, S24–S29. http://dx.doi.org/10.1192/bjp.bp.112.119180

Chemerinski, E., Triebwasser, J., Roussos, P., & Siever, L. J. (2013). Schizotypal personality disorder. *Journal of Personality Disorders*, *27*, 652–679. http://dx.doi.org/10.1521/pedi_2012_26_053

Chemtob, C. M., Hamada, R. S., Bauer, G., Torigoe, R. Y., & Kinney, B. (1988). Patient suicide: Frequency and impact on psychologists. *Professional Psychology: Research and Practice*, *19*, 416–420. http://dx.doi.org/10.1037/0735-7028.19.4.416

Choi-Kain, L. W., & Gunderson, J. G. (2008). Mentalization: Ontogeny, assessment, and application in the treatment of borderline personality disorder. *The American Journal of Psychiatry*, *165*, 1127–1135.

Cicchetti, D., & Rogosch, F. A. (1996). Equifinality and multifinality in developmental psychopathology. *Development and Psychopathology*, *8*, 597–600.

Cicchetti, D., & Rogosch, F. A. (2002). A developmental psychopathology perspective on adolescence. *Journal of Consulting and Clinical Psychology*, *70*, 6–20. http://dx.doi.org/10.1037/0022-006X.70.1.6

Clark, L. A. (2007). Assessment and diagnosis of personality disorder: Perennial issues and an emerging reconceptualization. *Annual Review of Psychology*, *58*, 227–257. http://dx.doi.org/10.1146/annurev.psych.57.102904.190200

Clarkin, J. F., Levy, K. N., Lenzenweger, M. F., & Kernberg, O. F. (2007). Evaluating three treatments for borderline personality disorder: A multiwave study. *The American Journal of Psychiatry*, *164*, 922–928.

Cleckley, H. (1964). *The mask of sanity* (4th ed.). St. Louis, MO: Mosby.

Cloninger, C. R., Sigvardsson, S., Bohman, M., & von Knorring, A.-L. (1982). Predisposition to petty criminality in Swedish adoptees: II. Cross-fostering analysis of gene–environment interaction. *Archives of General Psychiatry*, *39*, 1242–1247. http://dx.doi.org/10.1001/archpsyc.1982.04290110010002

Coccaro, E. F., Nayyer, H., & McCloskey, M. S. (2012). Personality disorder—not otherwise specified evidence of validity and consideration for *DSM–5*. *Comprehensive Psychiatry*, *53*, 907–914. http://dx.doi.org/10.1016/j.comppsych.2012.03.007

Cohen, P., & Cohen, J. (1984). The clinician's illusion. *Archives of General Psychiatry*, *41*, 1178–1182. http://dx.doi.org/10.1001/archpsyc.1984.01790230064010

Cohen, P., Crawford, T. N., Johnson, J. G., & Kasen, S. (2005). The children in the community study of developmental course of personality disorder. *Journal of Personality Disorders*, *19*, 466–486. http://dx.doi.org/10.1521/pedi.2005.19.5.466

Coid, J. (2009). Prevalence and correlates of psychopathic traits in the household population of Great Britain. *International Journal of Law and Psychiatry*, *32*, 65–73. http://dx.doi.org/10.1016/j.ijlp.2009.01.002

Coid, J., Yang, M., Tyrer, P., Roberts, A., & Ullrich, S. (2006). Prevalence and correlates of personality disorder in Great Britain. *The British Journal of Psychiatry*, *188*, 423–431. http://dx.doi.org/10.1192/bjp.188.5.423

Cooper, L. D., Balsis, S., & Oltmanns, T. F. (2012). Self- and informant-reported perspectives on symptoms of narcissistic personality disorder. *Personality Disorders: Theory, Research, and Treatment*, *3*, 140–154. http://dx.doi.org/10.1037/a0026576

Corrigan, P. W. (2000). Mental health stigma as social attribution: Implications for research methods and attitude change. *Clinical Psychology: Science and Practice*, *7*, 48–67. http://dx.doi.org/10.1093/clipsy.7.1.48

Crits-Christoph, P., Gibbons, M. C., & Mukherjee, D. (2013). Psychotherapy process–outcome research. In M. Lambert (Ed.), *Handbook of psychotherapy and behavior change* (pp. 298–340). New York, NY: Wiley.

Crowell, S. E., Beauchaine, T. P., & Linehan, M. M. (2009). A biosocial developmental model of borderline personality: Elaborating and extending Linehan's theory. *Psychological Bulletin*, *135*, 495–510. http://dx.doi.org/10.1037/a0015616

Davidson, K. M., & Tran, C. F. (2014). Impact of treatment intensity on suicidal behavior and depression in borderline personality disorder: A critical review. *Journal of Personality Disorders*, *28*, 181–197.

Davidson, K. M., Tyrer, P., Norrie, J., Palmer, S. J., & Tyrer, H. (2010). Cognitive therapy v. usual treatment for borderline personality disorder: Prospective 6-year follow-up. *The British Journal of Psychiatry, 197,* 456–462. http://dx.doi.org/10.1192/bjp.bp.109.074286

De Fruyt, F., & De Clercq, B. (2014). Antecedents of personality disorder in childhood and adolescence: Toward an integrative developmental model. *Annual Review of Clinical Psychology, 10,* 449–476. http://dx.doi.org/10.1146/annurev-clinpsy-032813-153634

de Rues, R. J. M., & Emmelkamp, P. M. G. (2012). Obsessive–compulsive personality disorder: A review of current empirical findings. *Personality and Mental Health, 6,* 1–21.

Dhawan, N., Kunik, M. E., Oldham, J., & Coverdale, J. (2010). Prevalence and treatment of narcissistic personality disorder in the community: A systematic review. *Comprehensive Psychiatry, 51,* 333–339. http://dx.doi.org/10.1016/j.comppsych.2009.09.003

Dimeff, L. A., & Linehan, M. M. (2008). Dialectical behavior therapy for substance abusers. *Addiction: Science and Clinical Practice, 4,* 39–47. http://dx.doi.org/10.1151/ascp084239

Disney, K. L. (2013). Dependent personality disorder: A critical review. *Clinical Psychology Review, 33,* 1184–1196. http://dx.doi.org/10.1016/j.cpr.2013.10.001

Dobbs, S. (2009, December). The science of success. *The Atlantic.* Retrieved from http://www.theatlantic.com/magazine/archive/2009/12/the-science-of-success/307761

Doering, S., Hörz, S., Rentrop, M., Fischer-Kern, M., Schuster, P., Benecke, C., . . . Buchheim, P. (2010). Transference-focused psychotherapy v. treatment by community psychotherapists for borderline personality disorder: Randomised controlled trial. *The British Journal of Psychiatry, 196,* 389–395. http://dx.doi.org/10.1192/bjp.bp.109.070177

Donegan, N. H., Sanislow, C. A., Blumberg, H. P., Fulbright, R. K., Lacadie, C., Skudlarski, P., . . . Wexler, B. E. (2003). Amygdala hyperreactivity in borderline personality disorder: Implications for emotional dysregulation. *Biological Psychiatry, 54,* 1284–1293. http://dx.doi.org/10.1016/S0006-3223(03)00636-X

Dunn, J., & Plomin, R. (1990). *Separate lives: Why siblings are so different.* New York, NY: Basic Books.

Engel, G. L. (1980). The clinical application of the biopsychosocial model. *The American Journal of Psychiatry, 137,* 535–544.

Fazel, S., & Danesh, J. (2002). Serious mental disorder in 23000 prisoners: A systematic review of 62 surveys. *The Lancet, 359,* 545–550. http://dx.doi.org/10.1016/S0140-6736(02)07740-1

Fergusson, D. M., & Mullen, P. E. (1999). *Childhood sexual abuse: An evidence-based perspective.* Thousand Oaks, CA: Sage.

Finkelhor, D., Ormrod, R., Turner, H., & Hamby, S. L. (2005). The victimization of children and youth: A comprehensive, national survey. *Child Maltreatment, 10,* 5–25. http://dx.doi.org/10.1177/1077559504271287

Forman, E. M., Berk, M. S., Henriques, G. R., Brown, G. K., & Beck, A. T. (2004). History of multiple suicide attempts as a behavioral marker of severe psychopathology. *The American Journal of Psychiatry, 161,* 437–443. http://dx.doi.org/10.1176/appi.ajp.161.3.437

Foster, J. D., Campbell, W. K., & Twenge, J. M. (2003). Individual differences in narcissism: Inflated self-views across the lifespan and around the world. *Journal of Research in Personality, 37,* 469–486. http://dx.doi.org/10.1016/S0092-6566(03)00026-6

Freud, S. (1962). Analysis terminable and interminable. In J. Strachey (Ed.), *The standard edition of the psychological works of Sigmund Freud* (Vol. 23, pp. 216–254). London, England: Hogarth Press. (Original work published 1937)

Fridell, M., Hesse, M., Jaeger, M. M., & Kühlhorn, E. (2008). Antisocial personality disorder as a predictor of criminal behaviour in a longitudinal study of a cohort of abusers of several classes of drugs: Relation to type of substance and type of crime. *Addictive Behaviors, 33,* 799–811. http://dx.doi.org/10.1016/j.addbeh.2008.01.001

Funtowicz, M. N., & Widiger, T. A. (1999). Sex bias in the diagnosis of personality disorders: An evaluation of the *DSM–IV* criteria. *Journal of Abnormal Psychology, 108,* 195–201. http://dx.doi.org/10.1037/0021-843X.108.2.195

Giesen-Bloo, J., van Dyck, R., Spinhoven, P., van Tilburg, W., Dirksen, C., van Asselt, T., . . . Arntz, A. (2006). Outpatient psychotherapy for borderline personality disorder: Randomized trial of schema-focused therapy vs transference-focused psychotherapy. *Archives of General Psychiatry, 63,* 649–658. http://dx.doi.org/10.1001/archpsyc.63.6.649

Gordon, T. (2000). *Parent effectiveness training: The proven program for raising responsible children.* New York, NY: Random House.

Grant, B. F., Hasin, D. S., Stinson, F. S., Dawson, D. A., Chou, S. P., Ruan, W. J., & Pickering, R. P. (2004). Prevalence, correlates, and disability of personality disorders in the United States: Results from the national epidemiologic survey on alcohol and related conditions. *Journal of Clinical Psychiatry, 65,* 948–958. http://dx.doi.org/10.4088/JCP.v65n0711

Gross, J. J. (2013). *Foundations of emotion regulation* (2nd ed.). New York, NY: Guilford Press.

Gunderson, J. G. (2013). *DSM–5:* Current status, lessons learned, and future challenges. *Psychotherapy: Theory, Research, & Practice, 4,* 368–376.

Gunderson, J. G., & Links, P. R. (2012). *Borderline personality disorder: A clinical guide* (2nd ed.). Washington, DC: American Psychiatric Publishing.

Gunderson, J. G., & Links, P. R. (2014). *Handbook of good psychiatric management for borderline personality disorder.* Washington, DC: American Psychiatric Publishing.

Gunderson, J. G., & Lyons-Ruth, K. (2008). BPD's interpersonal hypersensitivity phenotype: A gene–environment–developmental model. *Journal of Personality Disorders, 22,* 22–41. http://dx.doi.org/10.1521/pedi.2008.22.1.22

Gunderson, J. G., & Phillips, K. A. (1991). A current view of the interface between borderline personality disorder and depression. *The American Journal of Psychiatry, 148,* 967–975.

Gunderson, J. G., & Singer, M. T. (1975). Defining borderline patients: An overview. *The American Journal of Psychiatry, 132,* 1–10.

Gunderson, J. G., Stout, R. L., McGlashan, T. H., Shea, M. T., Morey, L. C., Grilo, C. M., . . . Skodol, A. E. (2011). Ten-year course of borderline personality disorder: Psychopathology and function from the Collaborative Longitudinal Personality Disorders study. *Archives of General Psychiatry, 68,* 827–837. http://dx.doi.org/10.1001/archgenpsychiatry.2011.37

Gutheil, T. G. (2004). Suicide, suicide litigation, and borderline personality disorder. *Journal of Personality Disorders, 18,* 248–256. http://dx.doi.org/10.1521/pedi.18.3.248.35448

Guzder, J., Paris, J., Zelkowitz, P., & Marchessault, K. (1996). Risk factors for borderline pathology in children. *Journal of the American Academy of Child & Adolescent Psychiatry, 35,* 26–33. http://dx.doi.org/10.1097/00004583-199601000-00009

Hare, R. D. (1999). *Without conscience: The disturbing world of the psychopaths among us.* New York, NY: Guilford Press.

Hare, R. D. (2003). *Manual for the Revised Psychopathy Checklist* (2nd ed.). Toronto, Ontario, Canada: Multi-Health Systems.

Herman, J. L. (1992). *Trauma and recovery.* New York, NY: Basic Books.

Hill, J. (2003). Early identification of individuals at risk for antisocial personality disorder. *The British Journal of Psychiatry, 44,* S11–S14. http://dx.doi.org/10.1192/bjp.182.44.s11

Hill, P. L., & Roberts, B. W. (2011). Examining "developmental me": A review of narcissism in a life span perspective. In W. K. Campbell & J. Miller (Eds.), *Handbook of narcissism and narcissistic personality disorder* (pp. 191–201). New York, NY: Wiley.

Hirschfeld, R. M. (1993). Personality disorders: Definition and diagnosis. *Journal of Personality Disorders*, Suppl. 7, 9–17.

Horton, R. S. (2011). Parenting and narcissism. In W. K. Campbell & J. Miller (Eds.), *Handbook of narcissism and narcissistic personality disorder* (pp. 181–190). New York, NY: Wiley.

Horton, R. S., Bleau, G., & Drwecki, B. (2006). Parenting narcissus: What are the links between parenting and narcissism? *Journal of Personality*, *74*, 345–376. http://dx.doi.org/10.1111/j.1467-6494.2005.00378.x

Horwitz, A. V., & Wakefield, J. C. (2007). *The loss of sadness: How psychiatry transformed normal sorrow into depressive disorder.* New York, NY: Oxford University Press.

Horwitz, A. V., & Wakefield, J. C. (2012). *All we have to fear: Psychiatry's transformation of natural anxieties into mental disorders.* New York, NY: Oxford University Press.

Horwitz, L. (1974). *Clinical prediction in psychotherapy.* New York, NY: Aronson.

Hwu, H. G., Yeh, E. K., & Chang, L. Y. (1989). Prevalence of psychiatric disorders in Taiwan defined by the Chinese Diagnostic Interview Schedule. *Acta Psychiatrica Scandinavica*, *79*, 136–147. http://dx.doi.org/10.1111/j.1600-0447.1989.tb08581.x

Hyman, S. E. (2010). The diagnosis of mental disorders: The problem of reification. *Annual Review of Clinical Psychology*, *6*, 155–179. http://dx.doi.org/10.1146/annurev.clinpsy.3.022806.091532

Ingenhoven, T., Lafay, P., Rinne, T., Passchier, J., & Duivenvoorden, H. (2010). Effectiveness of pharmacotherapy for severe personality disorders: Meta-analyses of randomized controlled trials. *Journal of Clinical Psychiatry*, *71*, 14–25. http://dx.doi.org/10.4088/JCP.08r04526gre

Insel, T., Cuthbert, B., Garvey, M., Heinssen, R., Pine, D. S., Quinn, K., . . . Wang, P. (2010). Research domain criteria (RDoC): Toward a new classification framework for research on mental disorders. *The American Journal of Psychiatry*, *167*, 748–751. http://dx.doi.org/10.1176/appi.ajp.2010.09091379

Insel, T. R., & Quirion, R. (2005). Psychiatry as a clinical neuroscience discipline. *JAMA*, *294*, 2221–2224. http://dx.doi.org/10.1001/jama.294.17.2221

Jones, E. E., & Harris, V. A. (1967). The attribution of attitudes. *Journal of Experimental Social Psychology*, *3*, 1–24. http://dx.doi.org/10.1016/0022-1031(67)90034-0

Jørgensen, C. R., Freund, C., Bøye, R., Jordet, H., Andersen, D., & Kjølbye, M. (2013). Outcome of mentalization-based and supportive psychotherapy in patients with borderline personality disorder: A randomized trial. *Acta Psychiatrica Scandinavica*, *127*, 305–317. http://dx.doi.org/10.1111/j.1600-0447.2012.01923.x

Kagan, J. (2004). *The long shadow of temperament.* Cambridge, MA: Harvard University Press.

Kagan, J. (2012). *Psychology's ghosts.* New Haven, CT: Yale University Press.

Kendall, T., Burbeck, R., & Bateman, A. (2010). Pharmacotherapy for borderline personality disorder: NICE guideline. *The British Journal of Psychiatry, 196,* 158–159. http://dx.doi.org/10.1192/bjp.196.2.158

Kendell, R. E. (2002). The distinction between personality disorder and mental illness. *The British Journal of Psychiatry, 180,* 110–115. http://dx.doi.org/10.1192/bjp.180.2.110

Kendler, K. S., Aggen, S. H., Czajkowski, N., Røysamb, E., Tambs, K., Torgersen, S., . . . Reichborn-Kjennerud, T. (2008). The structure of genetic and environmental risk factors for *DSM–IV* personality disorders: A multivariate twin study. *Archives of General Psychiatry, 65,* 1438–1446. http://dx.doi.org/10.1001/archpsyc.65.12.1438

Kendler, K. S., & Prescott, C. A. (2006). *Genes, environment, and psychopathology: Understanding the causes of psychiatric and substance use disorders.* New York, NY: Guilford Press.

Kerig, P. K., & Stellwagen, K. K. (2010). Roles of callous-unemotional traits, narcissism, and Machiavellianism in childhood aggression. *Journal of Psychopathology and Behavioral Assessment, 32,* 343–352. http://dx.doi.org/10.1007/s10862-009-9168-7

Kernberg, O. F. (1976). *Borderline conditions and pathological narcissism.* New York, NY: Aronson.

Kessler, R. C., Berglund, P., Borges, G., Nock, M., & Wang, P. S. (2005). Trends in suicide ideation, plans, gestures, and attempts in the United States, 1990–1992 to 2001–2003. *JAMA, 293,* 2487–2495. http://dx.doi.org/10.1001/jama.293.20.2487

Kirsch, I., Deacon, B. J., Huedo-Medina, T. B., Scoboria, A., Moore, T. J., & Johnson, B. T. (2008). Initial severity and antidepressant benefits: A meta-analysis of data submitted to the Food and Drug Administration. *PLoS Medicine, 5,* e45. http://dx.doi.org/10.1371/journal.pmed.0050045

Kliem, S., Kröger, C., & Kosfelder, J. (2010). Dialectical behavior therapy for borderline personality disorder: A meta-analysis using mixed-effects modeling. *Journal of Consulting and Clinical Psychology, 78,* 936–951. http://dx.doi.org/10.1037/a0021015

Klonsky, E. D. (2007). The functions of deliberate self-injury: A review of the evidence. *Clinical Psychology Review, 27,* 226–239. http://dx.doi.org/10.1016/j.cpr.2006.08.002

Koenigsberg, H. W. (2010). Affective instability: Toward an integration of neuroscience and psychological perspectives. *Journal of Personality Disorders, 24,* 60–82. http://dx.doi.org/10.1521/pedi.2010.24.1.60

Koenigsberg, H. W., Denny, B. T., Fan, J., Liu, X., Guerreri, S., Mayson, S. J., . . . Siever, L. J. (2014). The neural correlates of anomalous habituation to negative emotional pictures in borderline and avoidant personality disorder patients. *The American Journal of Psychiatry, 171,* 82–90. http://dx.doi.org/10.1176/appi.ajp.2013.13070852

Kohut, H. (1970). *The analysis of the self.* Madison, CT: International Universities Press.

Krueger, R. F., & Tackett, J. L. (Eds.). (2006). *Personality and Psychopathology.* New York, NY: Guilford Press.

Kupfer, D. J., & Regier, D. A. (2011). Neuroscience, clinical evidence, and the future of psychiatric classification in *DSM–5. The American Journal of Psychiatry, 168,* 672–674. http://dx.doi.org/10.1176/appi.ajp.2011.11020219

Laporte, L., Paris, J., Guttman, H., & Russell, J. (2011). Psychopathology, childhood trauma, and personality traits in patients with borderline personality disorder and their sisters. *Journal of Personality Disorders, 25,* 448–462. http://dx.doi.org/10.1521/pedi.2011.25.4.448

Laporte, L., Paris, J., Russell, J., Guttman, H., & Correa, J. (2012). Using a sibling design to compare childhood adversities in female patients with BPD and their sisters. *Child Maltreatment, 17,* 318–329. http://dx.doi.org/10.1177/1077559512461173

Lasch, C. (1979). *The culture of narcissism.* New York, NY: Warner.

Lenzenweger, M. F. (1999). Stability and change in personality disorder features: The Longitudinal Study of Personality Disorders. *Archives of General Psychiatry, 56,* 1009–1015. http://dx.doi.org/10.1001/archpsyc.56.11.1009

Lenzenweger, M. F., Lane, M. C., Loranger, A. W., & Kessler, R. C. (2007). *DSM–IV* personality disorders in the National Comorbidity Survey Replication. *Biological Psychiatry, 62,* 553–564. http://dx.doi.org/10.1016/j.biopsych.2006.09.019

Lesage, A. D., Boyer, R., Grunberg, F., Vanier, C., Morissette, R., Ménard-Buteau, C., & Loyer, M. (1994). Suicide and mental disorders: A case–control study of young men. *The American Journal of Psychiatry, 151,* 1063–1068.

Linehan, M. M. (1993). *Dialectical behavior therapy for borderline personality disorder.* New York, NY: Guilford Press.

Linehan, M. M. (2014). *DBT skills training manual* (2nd ed.). New York, NY: Guilford Press.

Linehan, M. M., Armstrong, H. E., Suarez, A., Allmon, D., & Heard, H. L. (1991). Cognitive-behavioral treatment of chronically parasuicidal borderline patients. *Archives of General Psychiatry, 48,* 1060–1064. http://dx.doi.org/10.1001/archpsyc.1991.01810360024003

Linehan, M. M., Comtois, K. A., Murray, A. M., Brown, M. Z., Gallop, R. J., Heard, H. L., . . . Lindenboim, N. (2006). Two-year randomized controlled trial and follow-up of dialectical behavior therapy vs therapy by experts for suicidal behaviors and borderline personality disorder. *Archives of General Psychiatry, 63,* 757–766. http://dx.doi.org/10.1001/archpsyc.63.7.757

Linehan, M. M., & Koerner, K. (2012). *Dialectical behavior therapy—A practical guide.* New York, NY: Guilford Press.

Livesley, W. J. (2003). *The practical management of personality disorder.* New York, NY: Guilford Press.

Livesley, W. J. (2010). Confusion and incoherence in the classification of personality disorder: Commentary on the preliminary proposals for *DSM–5. Psychological Injury and Law, 3,* 304–313. http://dx.doi.org/10.1007/s12207-010-9094-8

Livesley, W. J. (2012). Integrated treatment: A conceptual framework for an evidence-based approach to the treatment of personality disorder. *Journal of Personality Disorders, 26,* 17–42.

Livesley, W. J., Jang, K. L., & Vernon, P. A. (1998). Phenotypic and genetic structure of traits delineating personality disorder. *Archives of General Psychiatry, 55,* 941–948. http://dx.doi.org/10.1001/archpsyc.55.10.941

Lopez-Castroman, J., Galfalvy, H., Currier, D., Stanley, B., Blasco-Fontecilla, H., Baca-Garcia, E., . . . Oquendo, M. A. (2012). Personality disorder assessments in acute depressive episodes: Stability at follow-up. *Journal of Nervous and Mental Disease, 200,* 526–530. http://dx.doi.org/10.1097/NMD.0b013e318257c6ab

Maltsberger, J. T. (1994). Calculated risks in the treatment of intractably suicidal patients. *Psychiatry: Interpersonal and Biological Processes, 57,* 199–212.

Mauchnik, J., & Schmahl, C. (2010). The latest neuroimaging findings in borderline personality disorder. *Current Psychiatry Reports, 12,* 46–55. http://dx.doi.org/10.1007/s11920-009-0089-7

McGirr, A., Paris, J., Lesage, A., Renaud, J., & Turecki, G. (2007). Risk factors for suicide completion in borderline personality disorder: A case–control study of cluster B comorbidity and impulsive aggression. *Journal of Clinical Psychiatry, 68,* 721–729. http://dx.doi.org/10.4088/JCP.v68n0509

McGlashan, T. H. (1986). The Chestnut Lodge follow-up study. III. Long-term outcome of borderline personalities. *Archives of General Psychiatry, 43,* 20–30. http://dx.doi.org/10.1001/archpsyc.1986.01800010022003

McGrath, R. E. (2010). Prescriptive authority for psychologists. *Annual Review of Clinical Psychology, 6,* 21–47. http://dx.doi.org/10.1146/annurev-clinpsy-090209-151448

McMain, S. F., Links, P. S., Gnam, W. H., Guimond, T., Cardish, R. J., Korman, L., & Streiner, D. L. (2009). A randomized trial of dialectical behavior therapy versus general psychiatric management for borderline personality disorder.

The American Journal of Psychiatry, 166, 1365–1374. http://dx.doi.org/10.1176/appi.ajp.2009.09010039

McNally, R. J. (2003). *Remembering trauma.* Cambridge, MA: Belknap Press/Harvard University Press.

Mednick, S. A., Moffitt, T. E., & Stack, S. A. (Eds.). (2009). *The causes of crime: New biological approaches.* New York, NY: Academic Press.

Miller, J. D., & Campbell, W. K. (2010). The case for using research on trait narcissism as a building block for understanding narcissistic personality disorder. *Personality Disorders: Theory, Research, and Treatment, 1*, 180–191. http://dx.doi.org/10.1037/a0018229

Miller, J. D., Gaughan, E. T., Pryor, L. R., Kamen, C., & Campbell, W. K. (2009). Is research using the narcissistic personality inventory relevant for understanding narcissistic personality disorder? *Journal of Research in Personality, 43*, 482–488. http://dx.doi.org/10.1016/j.jrp.2009.02.001

Miller, J. D., Hoffman, B. J., Campbell, W. K., & Pilkonis, P. A. (2008). An examination of the factor structure of *Diagnostic and Statistical Manual of Mental Disorders, Fourth Edition*, narcissistic personality disorder criteria: One or two factors? *Comprehensive Psychiatry, 49*, 141–145.

Miller, J. D., & Maples, J. (2012). Trait personality models of narcissistic personality disorder, grandiose narcissism, and vulnerable narcissism. In W. K. Campbell & J. Miller (Eds.), *Handbook of narcissism and narcissistic personality disorder* (pp. 71–88). New York, NY: Wiley. http://dx.doi.org/10.1002/9781118093108.ch7

Miller, W. R., & Rollnick, S. (2013). *Motivational interviewing: Helping people change* (3rd ed.). New York, NY: Guilford Press

Millon, T. (1993). Borderline personality disorder: A psychosocial epidemic. In J. Paris (Ed.), *Borderline personality disorder: Etiology and treatment* (pp. 197–210). Washington, DC: American Psychiatric Press.

Millon, T., & Davis, R. D. (2011). *Disorders of personality: DSM–IV and beyond* (3rd ed.). New York, NY: Wiley. http://dx.doi.org/10.1002/9781118099254

Moeller, F. G., Barratt, E. S., Dougherty, D. M., Schmitz, J. M., & Swann, A. C. (2001). Psychiatric aspects of impulsivity. *The American Journal of Psychiatry, 158*, 1783–1793. http://dx.doi.org/10.1176/appi.ajp.158.11.1783

Moffitt, T. E. (1993). Adolescence-limited and life-course-persistent antisocial behavior: A developmental taxonomy. *Psychological Review, 100*, 674–701. http://dx.doi.org/10.1037/0033-295X.100.4.674

Moffitt, T. E., Caspi, A., Taylor, A., Kokaua, J., Milne, B. J., Polanczyk, G., & Poulton, R. (2010). How common are common mental disorders? Evidence that lifetime prevalence rates are doubled by prospective versus retrospective ascertainment. *Psychological Medicine, 40,* 899–909. http://dx.doi.org/10.1017/S0033291709991036

Mojtabai, R., & Olfson, M. (2008). National trends in psychotherapy by office-based psychiatrists. *Archives of General Psychiatry, 65,* 962–970. http://dx.doi.org/10.1001/archpsyc.65.8.962

Mojtabai, R., & Olfson, M. (2011). Proportion of antidepressants prescribed without a psychiatric diagnosis is growing. *Health Affairs, 30,* 1434–1442. http://dx.doi.org/10.1377/hlthaff.2010.1024

Monroe, S. M., & Simons, A. D. (1991). Diathesis-stress theories in the context of life stress research: Implications for the depressive disorders. *Psychological Bulletin, 110,* 406–425. http://dx.doi.org/10.1037/0033-2909.110.3.406

Moore, M., Yuen, H. M., Dunn, N., Mullee, M. A., Maskell, J., & Kendrick, T. (2009). Explaining the rise in antidepressant prescribing: A descriptive study using the general practice research database. *BMJ: British Medical Journal, 339,* b3999. http://dx.doi.org/10.1136/bmj.b3999

Moran, P. (1999). The epidemiology of antisocial personality disorder. *Social Psychiatry and Psychiatric Epidemiology, 34,* 231–242. http://dx.doi.org/10.1007/s001270050138

Moran, P., Coffey, C., Romaniuk, H., Olsson, C., Borschmann, R., Carlin, J. B., & Patton, G. C. (2012). The natural history of self-harm from adolescence to young adulthood: A population-based cohort study. *The Lancet, 379,* 236–243. http://dx.doi.org/10.1016/S0140-6736(11)61141-0

Morey, L. C., Hopwood, C. J., Gunderson, J. G., Skodol, A. E., Shea, M. T., Yen, S., . . . McGlashan, T. H. (2007). Comparison of alternative models for personality disorders. *Psychological Medicine, 37,* 983–994. http://dx.doi.org/10.1017/S0033291706009482

Morey, L. C., Krueger, R. F., & Skodol, A. E. (2013). The hierarchical structure of clinician ratings of proposed *DSM–5* pathological personality traits. *Journal of Abnormal Psychology, 122,* 836–841. http://dx.doi.org/10.1037/a0034003

Morey, L. C., & Zanarini, M. C. (2000). Borderline personality: Traits and disorder. *Journal of Abnormal Psychology, 109,* 733–737. http://dx.doi.org/10.1037/0021-843X.109.4.733

Mullen, P. E. (2007). Dangerous and severe personality disorder and in need of treatment. *British Journal of Psychiatry Supplement, 49,* s3–s7. http://dx.doi.org/10.1192/bjp.190.5.s3

New, A. S., Goodman, M., Triebwasser, J., & Siever, L. J. (2008). Recent advances in the biological study of personality disorders. *Psychiatric Clinics of North America, 31,* 441–461, vii. http://dx.doi.org/10.1016/j.psc.2008.03.011

Newcomer, J. W., & Haupt, D. W. (2006). The metabolic effects of antipsychotic medications. *Canadian Journal of Psychiatry, 51,* 480–491.

Newton-Howes, G., Tyrer, P., & Johnson, T. (2006). Personality disorder and the outcome of depression: Meta-analysis of published studies. *The British Journal of Psychiatry, 188*, 13–20. http://dx.doi.org/10.1192/bjp.188.1.13

Ni, X., Chan, D., Chan, K., McMain, S., & Kennedy, J. L. (2009). Serotonin genes and gene-gene interactions in borderline personality disorder in a matched case–control study. *Progress in Neuro-Psychopharmacology & Biological Psychiatry, 33*, 128–133. http://dx.doi.org/10.1016/j.pnpbp.2008.10.022

Nurnberg, G., Raskin, M., Levine, P. E., Pollack, S., Siegel, O., & Prince, R. (1991). The comorbidity of borderline personality disorder with other *DSM–III–R* Axis II personality disorders. *The American Journal of Psychiatry, 148*, 1311–1317.

Ogrodniczuk, J. S. (Ed.). (2013). *Understanding and treating pathological narcissism.* Washington, DC: American Psychological Association. http://dx.doi.org/10.1037/14041-000

Osler, W. (1898). *The principles and practice of medicine.* New York, NY: Appleton.

Paris, J. (1998). *Working with traits: Psychotherapy of personality disorders.* Northvale, NJ: Aronson.

Paris, J. (2000). *Myths of childhood.* Philadelphia, PA: Brunner/Mazel.

Paris, J. (2003). *Personality disorders over time: Precursors, course, and outcome.* Washington, DC: American Psychiatric Press.

Paris, J. (2006). *Half in love with death: Managing the chronically suicidal patient.* Mahwah, NJ: Laurence Erlbaum.

Paris, J. (2007a). The nature of borderline personality disorder: Multiple dimensions, multiple symptoms, but one category. *Journal of Personality Disorders, 21*, 457–473. http://dx.doi.org/10.1521/pedi.2007.21.5.457

Paris, J. (2007b). Intermittent psychotherapy: An alternative to continuous long-term treatment for patients with personality disorders. *Journal of Psychiatric Practice, 13*, 153–158. http://dx.doi.org/10.1097/01.pra.0000271656.09717.ab

Paris, J. (2007c). The nature of borderline personality disorder: Multiple dimensions, multiple symptoms, but one category. *Journal of Personality Disorders, 21*, 457–473. http://dx.doi.org/10.1521/pedi.2007.21.5.457

Paris, J. (2008a). *Treatment of borderline personality disorder: A guide to evidence-based practice.* New York, NY: Guilford Press.

Paris, J. (2008b). *Prescriptions for the mind.* New York, NY: Oxford University Press.

Paris, J. (2010a). Estimating the prevalence of personality disorders in the community. *Journal of Personality Disorders, 24*, 405–411. http://dx.doi.org/10.1521/pedi.2010.24.4.405

Paris, J. (2010b). Effectiveness of different psychotherapy approaches in the treatment of borderline personality disorder. *Current Psychiatry Reports, 12*, 56–60. http://dx.doi.org/10.1007/s11920-009-0083-0

Paris, J. (2010c). *The use and misuse of psychiatric drugs: An evidence-based guide.* Chichester, England: Wiley. http://dx.doi.org/10.1002/9780470666630

Paris, J. (2012). *The bipolar spectrum: Diagnosis or fad?* New York, NY: Routledge.

Paris, J. (2013a). *The intelligent clinician's guide to the DSM–5.* New York, NY: Oxford University Press. http://dx.doi.org/10.1093/med/9780199738175.001.0001

Paris, J. (2013b). *Psychotherapy in an age of narcissism.* Hampton, England: Palgrave MacMillan.

Paris, J. (2013c). Stepped care: An alternative to routine extended treatment for patients with borderline personality disorder. *Psychiatric Services, 64,* 1035–1037. http://dx.doi.org/10.1176/appi.ps.201200451

Paris, J. (2013d). *Fads and fallacies in psychiatry.* London, England: Royal College of Psychiatrists.

Paris, J. (2014a). Modernity and narcissistic personality disorder. *Personality Disorders: Theory, Research, and Treatment, 5,* 220–226

Paris, J. (2014b). Social capital and personality disorders. *Personality and Mental Health, 8,* 24–29.

Paris, J. (in press). Applying the principles of psychotherapy integration to the treatment of borderline personality disorder. *Journal of Psychotherapy Integration.*

Paris, J., Brown, R., & Nowlis, D. (1987). Long-term follow-up of borderline patients in a general hospital. *Comprehensive Psychiatry, 28,* 530–535. http://dx.doi.org/10.1016/0010-440X(87)90019-8

Paris, J., Chenard-Poirier, M.-P., & Biskin, R. (2013). Antisocial and borderline personality disorders revisited. *Comprehensive Psychiatry, 54,* 321–325. http://dx.doi.org/10.1016/j.comppsych.2012.10.006

Paris, J., Gunderson, J., & Weinberg, I. (2007). The interface between borderline personality disorder and bipolar spectrum disorders. *Comprehensive Psychiatry, 48,* 145–154. http://dx.doi.org/10.1016/j.comppsych.2006.10.001

Paris, J., & Lis, E. (2013). Can sociocultural and historical mechanisms influence the development of borderline personality disorder? *Transcultural Psychiatry, 50,* 140–151. http://dx.doi.org/10.1177/1363461512468105

Paris, J., & Zweig-Frank, H. (2001). A 27-year follow-up of patients with borderline personality disorder. *Comprehensive Psychiatry, 42,* 482–487. http://dx.doi.org/10.1053/comp.2001.26271

Paris, J., Zweig-Frank, H., & Guzder, J. (1994a). Psychological risk factors for borderline personality disorder in female patients. *Comprehensive Psychiatry, 35,* 301–305. http://dx.doi.org/10.1016/0010-440X(94)90023-X

Paris, J., Zweig-Frank, H., & Guzder, J. (1994b). Risk factors for borderline personality in male outpatients. *Journal of Nervous and Mental Disease, 182,* 375–380. http://dx.doi.org/10.1097/00005053-199407000-00002

Park, H., Twenge, J. M., & Greenfield, P. M. (2014). The great recession: Implications for adolescent values and behavior. *Social Psychological and Personality Science, 5,* 310–318.

Parker, G. (1983). *Parental overprotection: A risk factor in psychosocial development.* New York, NY: Grune and Stratton.

Perry, J. C. (1992). Problems and considerations in the valid assessment of personality disorders. *The American Journal of Psychiatry, 149,* 1645–1653.

Pincus, A. L., & Lukowitsky, M. R. (2010). Pathological narcissism and narcissistic personality disorder. *Annual Review of Clinical Psychology, 6,* 421–446. http://dx.doi.org/10.1146/annurev.clinpsy.121208.131215

Piper, W. E., Rosie, J. S., & Joyce, A. S. (1996). *Time-limited day treatment for personality disorders: Integration of research and practice in a group program.* Washington, DC: American Psychological Association.

Plakun, E. M., Burkhardt, P. E., & Muller, J. P. (1985). 14-year follow-up of borderline and schizotypal personality disorders. *Comprehensive Psychiatry, 26,* 448–455. http://dx.doi.org/10.1016/0010-440X(85)90081-1

Plomin, R., DeFries, J. C., Knopik, V. S., & Neiderhiser, J. M. (2012). *Behavioral genetics* (6th ed.). London, England: Worth.

Pratt, L. A., Brody, D. J., & Gu, Q. (2011). *Antidepressant use in persons aged 12 and over: United States, 2005–2008* (NCHS data brief, no. 76). Hyattsville, MD: National Center for Health Statistics.

Raine, A. (2013). *The anatomy of violence.* New York, NY: Oxford University Press.

Réale, D., Reader, S. M., Sol, D., McDougall, P. T., & Dingemanse, N. J. (2007). Integrating animal temperament within ecology and evolution. *Biological Reviews of the Cambridge Philosophical Society, 82,* 291–318. http://dx.doi.org/10.1111/j.1469-185X.2007.00010.x

Regier, D. A., Narrow, W. E., Clarke, D. E., Kraemer, H. C., Kuramoto, S. J., Kuhl, E. A., & Kupfer, D. J. (2013). *DSM–5* field trials in the United States and Canada, Part II: Test-retest reliability of selected categorical diagnoses. *The American Journal of Psychiatry, 170,* 59–70. http://dx.doi.org/10.1176/appi.ajp.2012.12070999

Reichborn-Kjennerud, T., Ystrom, E., Neale, M. C., Aggen, S. H., Mazzeo, S. E., Knudsen, G. P., . . . Kendler, K. S. (2013). Structure of genetic and environmental risk factors for symptoms of *DSM–IV* borderline personality disorder. *JAMA Psychiatry, 70,* 1206–1214. http://dx.doi.org/10.1001/jamapsychiatry.2013.1944

Rettew, D. C., & McKee, L. (2005). Temperament and its role in developmental psychopathology. *Harvard Review of Psychiatry, 13,* 14–27. http://dx.doi.org/10.1080/10673220590923146

Robins, L. N. (1966). *Deviant children grown up*. Baltimore, MD: Williams and Wilkins.

Robins, L. N., & Regier, D. A. (Eds.). (1991). *Psychiatric disorders in America*. New York, NY: Free Press.

Ronningstam, E. (2010). Narcissistic personality disorder: A current review. *Current Psychiatry Reports, 12*, 68–75. http://dx.doi.org/10.1007/s11920-009-0084-z

Ronningstam, E. (2011). Narcissistic personality disorder: A clinical perspective. *Journal of Psychiatric Practice, 17*, 89–99. http://dx.doi.org/10.1097/01.pra.0000396060.67150.40

Rosenbluth, M., & Sinyor, M. (2012). Off-label use of atypical antipsychotics in personality disorders. *Expert Opinion on Pharmacotherapy, 13*, 1575–1585. http://dx.doi.org/10.1517/14656566.2011.608351

Rothbart, M. K. (2007). Temperament, development and personality. *Current Directions in Psychological Science, 16*, 207–212. http://dx.doi.org/10.1111/j.1467-8721.2007.00505.x

Røysamb, E., Kendler, K. S., Tambs, K., Orstavik, R. E., Neale, M. C., Aggen, S. H., . . . Reichborn-Kjennerud, T. (2011). The joint structure of *DSM–IV* Axis I and Axis II disorders. *Journal of Abnormal Psychology, 120*, 198–209. http://dx.doi.org/10.1037/a0021660

Ruocco, A. C. (2005). The neuropsychology of borderline personality disorder: A meta-analysis and review. *Psychiatry Research, 137*, 191–202. http://dx.doi.org/10.1016/j.psychres.2005.07.004

Ruocco, A. C., Amirthavasagam, S., & Zakzanis, K. K. (2012). Amygdala and hippocampal volume reductions as candidate endophenotypes for borderline personality disorder: A meta-analysis of magnetic resonance imaging studies. *Psychiatry Research: Neuroimaging, 201*, 245–252. http://dx.doi.org/10.1016/j.pscychresns.2012.02.012

Russell, J. J., Moskowitz, D. S., Zuroff, D. C., Sookman, D., & Paris, J. (2007). Stability and variability of affective experience and interpersonal behavior in borderline personality disorder. *Journal of Abnormal Psychology, 116*, 578–588. http://dx.doi.org/10.1037/0021-843X.116.3.578

Rutter, M. (1987). Temperament, personality and personality disorder. *The British Journal of Psychiatry, 150*, 443–458. http://dx.doi.org/10.1192/bjp.150.4.443

Rutter, M. (2006). *Genes and behavior: Nature–nurture interplay explained*. London, England: Blackwell.

Rutter, M. (2012). Resilience as a dynamic concept. *Development and Psychopathology, 24*, 335–344. http://dx.doi.org/10.1017/S0954579412000028

Rutter, M., & Rutter, M. (1993). *Developing minds: Challenge and continuity across the life span*. New York, NY: Basic Books.

Rutter, M., & Smith, D. J. (1995). *Psychosocial problems in young people.* Cambridge, England: Cambridge University Press.

Samuel, D. B., & Widiger, T. A. (2011). Conscientiousness and obsessive–compulsive personality disorder. *Personality Disorders: Theory, Research, and Treatment, 2,* 161–174. http://dx.doi.org/10.1037/a0021216

Sanislow, C. A., da Cruz, K., Gianoli, M. O., & Reagan, E. R. (2012). Avoidant personality disorder, traits, and type. In T. A. Widiger (Ed.), *The Oxford handbook of personality disorders* (pp. 549–565). New York, NY: Oxford University Press.

Saulsman, L. M., & Page, A. C. (2004). The five-factor model and personality disorder empirical literature: A meta-analytic review. *Clinical Psychology Review, 23,* 1055–1085. http://dx.doi.org/10.1016/j.cpr.2002.09.001

Scott, L. N., Stepp, S. D., & Pilkonis, P. A. (2014). Prospective associations between features of borderline personality disorder, emotion dysregulation, and aggression. *Personality Disorders: Theory, Research, and Treatment, 5,* 278–288. http://dx.doi.org/10.1037/per0000070

Scull, A. (2009). *Hysteria: The biography.* New York, NY: Oxford University Press.

Shedler, J., Beck, A., Fonagy, P., Gabbard, G. O., Gunderson, J., Kernberg, O., . . . Westen, D. (2010). Personality disorders in *DSM–5. The American Journal of Psychiatry, 167,* 1026–1028. http://dx.doi.org/10.1176/appi.ajp.2010.10050746

Shorter, E. (1997). *A history of psychiatry: From the era of the asylum to the age of Prozac.* Oxford, England: John Wiley & Sons.

Siever, L. J., & Davis, K. L. (1991). A psychobiological perspective on the personality disorders. *The American Journal of Psychiatry, 148,* 1647–1658.

Simms, L. J., & Clark, L. A. (2006). The Schedule for Nonadaptive and Adaptive Personality (SNAP): A dimensional measure of traits relevant to personality and personality pathology. In S. Strack (Ed.), *Differentiating normal and abnormal personality* (pp. 431–450). New York, NY: Springer.

Skodol, A. E., Bender, D. S., Morey, L. C., Alarcon, R. D., Siever, L. J., Clark, L. A., . . . Oldham, J. M. (2011). Proposed changes in personality and personality disorder assessment and diagnosis for *DSM-5* Part I: Description and rationale. *Personality Disorders: Theory, Research, and Treatment, 2,* 4–22. http://dx.doi.org/10.1037/a0021891

Skodol, A. E., Buckley, P., & Charles, E. (1983). Is there a characteristic pattern to the treatment history of clinic outpatients with borderline personality? *Journal of Nervous and Mental Disease, 171,* 405–410. http://dx.doi.org/10.1097/00005053-198307000-00003

Skodol, A. E., Gunderson, J. G., Shea, M. T., McGlashan, T. H., Morey, L. C., Sanislow, C. A., . . . Stout, R. L. (2005). The collaborative longitudinal personality disorders study (CLPS): Overview and implications. *Journal of Personality Disorders, 19,* 487–504. http://dx.doi.org/10.1521/pedi.2005.19.5.487

Soloff, P. H., Lynch, K. G., & Kelly, T. M. (2002). Childhood abuse as a risk factor for suicidal behavior in borderline personality disorder. *Journal of Personality Disorders, 16,* 201–214. http://dx.doi.org/10.1521/pedi.16.3.201.22542

Soloff, P. H., Lynch, K. G., Kelly, T. M., Malone, K. M., & Mann, J. J. (2000). Characteristics of suicide attempts of patients with major depressive episode and borderline personality disorder: A comparative study. *The American Journal of Psychiatry, 157,* 601–608. http://dx.doi.org/10.1176/appi.ajp.157.4.601

Stanley, B., Brodsky, B., Nelson, J., & Dulit, R. (2007). Brief dialectical behavior therapy (DBT–B) for suicidal behavior and nonsuicidal self-injury. *Archives of Suicide Research, 11,* 337–341. http://dx.doi.org/10.1080/13811110701542069

Stepp, S. D., Pilkonis, P. A., Hipwell, A. E., Loeber, R., & Stouthamer-Loeber, M. (2010). Stability of borderline personality disorder features in girls. *Journal of Personality Disorders, 24,* 460–472. http://dx.doi.org/10.1521/pedi.2010.24.4.460

Stern, A. (1938). Psychoanalytic investigation of and therapy in the borderline group of neuroses. *The Psychoanalytic Quarterly, 7,* 467–489.

Stinson, F. S., Dawson, D. A., Goldstein, R. B., Chou, S. P., Huang, B., Smith, S. M., . . . Grant, B. F. (2008). Prevalence, correlates, disability, and comorbidity of *DSM–IV* narcissistic personality disorder: Results from the Wave 2 National Epidemiologic Survey on Alcohol and Related Conditions. *Journal of Clinical Psychiatry, 69,* 1033–1045. http://dx.doi.org/10.4088/JCP.v69n0701

Stoffers, J. M., Ferriter, M., Völlm, B. A., Gibbon, S., Jones, H. F., Duggan, C., . . . Lieb, K. (2012). Psychological interventions for people with histrionic personality disorder. *Cochrane Database of Systematic Reviews.* Advance online publication.

Stoffers, J. M., Völlm, B. A., Rücker, G., Timmer, A., Huband, N., & Lieb, K. (2010). Pharmacological interventions for borderline personality disorder. *Cochrane Database of Systematic Reviews, 6,* CD005653.

Stoffers, J. M., Völlm, B. A., Rücker, G., Timmer, A., Huband, N., & Lieb, K. (2012). Psychological therapies for people with borderline personality disorder. *Cochrane Database of Systematic Reviews, 8,* CD005652.

Stone, M. H. (1990). *The fate of borderline patients.* New York, NY: Guilford Press.

Strupp, H. H., Fox, R. E., & Lesser, K. (1969). *Patients view their psychotherapy.* Baltimore, MD: Johns Hopkins.

Tackett, J. L., Herzhoff, K., Reardon, K. W., De Clercq, B., & Sharp, C. (2014). The externalizing spectrum in youth: Incorporating personality pathology. *Journal of Adolescence, 37,* 659–668. http://dx.doi.org/10.1016/j.adolescence.2013.10.009

Tackett, J. L., & Mackrell, S. (2011). Narcissism and Machiavellianism in youth: Implications for the development of adaptive and maladaptive behavior. In C. T. Barry, P. K. Kerig, & K. K. Stellwagen (Eds.), *Narcissism and Machiavellianism in youth* (pp. 11–23). Washington, DC: American Psychological Association. http://dx.doi.org/10.1037/12352-001

Tackett, J. L., & Sharp, C. (2014). A developmental psychopathology perspective on personality disorder: Introduction to the special issue. *Journal of Personality Disorders, 28,* 1–4. http://dx.doi.org/10.1521/pedi.2014.28.1.1

Thomaes, S., Stegge, H., Bushman, B. J., Olthof, T., & Denissen, J. (2008). Development and validation of the childhood narcissism scale. *Journal of Personality Assessment, 90,* 382–391. http://dx.doi.org/10.1080/00223890802108162

Torgersen, S., Kringlen, E., & Cramer, V. (2001). The prevalence of personality disorders in a community sample. *Archives of General Psychiatry, 58,* 590–596. http://dx.doi.org/10.1001/archpsyc.58.6.590

Torgersen, S., Lygren, S., Oien, P. A., Skre, I., Onstad, S., Edvardsen, J., ... Kringlen, E. (2000). A twin study of personality disorders. *Comprehensive Psychiatry, 41,* 416–425. http://dx.doi.org/10.1053/comp.2000.16560

Tremblay, R. E. (2006). Prevention of youth violence: Why not start at the beginning? *Journal of Abnormal Child Psychology, 34,* 480–487. http://dx.doi.org/10.1007/s10802-006-9038-7

Trull, T. J., Jahng, S., Tomko, R. L., Wood, P. K., & Sher, K. J. (2010). Revised NESARC personality disorder diagnoses: Gender, prevalence, and comorbidity with substance dependence disorders. *Journal of Personality Disorders, 24,* 412–426. http://dx.doi.org/10.1521/pedi.2010.24.4.412

Trull, T. J., & Prinstein, M. (2012). *Clinical psychology.* Belmont, CA: Wadsworth.

Trull, T. J., Solhan, M. B., Tragesser, S. L., Jahng, S., Wood, P. K., Piasecki, T. M., & Watson, D. (2008). Affective instability: Measuring a core feature of borderline personality disorder with ecological momentary assessment. *Journal of Abnormal Psychology, 117,* 647–661. http://dx.doi.org/10.1037/a0012532

Twenge, J. M. (2011). Culture and narcissism. In W. K. Campbell & J. Miller (Eds.), *Handbook of narcissism and narcissistic personality disorder* (pp. 202–209). New York, NY: Wiley.

Twenge, J. M., & Campbell, W. K. (2009). *The narcissism epidemic: Living in the age of entitlement.* New York, NY: Simon & Schuster.

Tyrer, P., Crawford, M., Mulder, R., & the *ICD–11* Working Group for the Revision of Classification of Personality Disorders. (2011). Reclassifying personality disorders. *Lancet, 377,* 1814–1815. http://dx.doi.org/10.1016/S0140-6736(10)61926-5

Uher, R., & Rutter, M. (2012). Basing psychiatric classification on scientific foundation: Problems and prospects. *International Review of Psychiatry, 24,* 591–605. http://dx.doi.org/10.3109/09540261.2012.721346

Ullrich, S., & Coid, J. (2009). Antisocial personality disorder: Comorbid Axis I mental disorders and health service use among a national household population. *Personality and Mental Health, 3*, 151–164. http://dx.doi.org/10.1002/pmh.70

Valenstein, M. (2006). Keeping our eyes on STAR*D. *The American Journal of Psychiatry, 163*, 1484–1486.

Verheul, R., Bartak, A., & Widiger, T. (2007). Prevalence and construct validity of personality disorder not otherwise specified (PDNOS). *Journal of Personality Disorders, 21*, 359–370. http://dx.doi.org/10.1521/pedi.2007.21.4.359

Vernon, P. A., Villani, V. C., Vickers, L. C., & Harris, J. A. (2008). A behavioral genetic investigation of the Dark Triad and the Big 5. *Personality and Individual Differences, 44*, 445–452. http://dx.doi.org/10.1016/j.paid.2007.09.007

Wakefield, J. C. (1992). Disorder as harmful dysfunction: A conceptual critique of *DSM–III–R*'s definition of mental disorder. *Psychological Review, 99*, 232–247. http://dx.doi.org/10.1037/0033-295X.99.2.232

Wampold, B. E. (2001). *The great psychotherapy debate: Models, methods, and findings.* Mahwah, NJ: Erlbaum Associates.

White, C. N., Gunderson, J. G., Zanarini, M. C., & Hudson, J. I. (2003). Family studies of borderline personality disorder: A review. *Harvard Review of Psychiatry, 11*, 8–19.

Widiger, T. A. (2013). A postmortem and future look at the personality disorders in *DSM–5. Personality Disorders: Theory, Research, and Treatment, 4*, 382–387. http://dx.doi.org/10.1037/per0000030

Widiger, T. A., & Costa, P. T., Jr., (Eds.). (2013). *Personality disorders and the five-factor model of personality* (3rd ed.). Washington, DC: American Psychological Association.

Widiger, T. A., & Mullins-Sweatt, S. N. (2009). Five-factor model of personality disorder: A proposal for *DSM–V. Annual Review of Clinical Psychology, 5*, 197–220. http://dx.doi.org/10.1146/annurev.clinpsy.032408.153542

Wilberg, T., Hummelen, B., Pedersen, G., & Karterud, S. (2008). A study of patients with personality disorder not otherwise specified. *Comprehensive Psychiatry, 49*, 460–468. http://dx.doi.org/10.1016/j.comppsych.2007.12.008

Woody, G. E., McLellan, A. T., Luborsky, L., & O'Brien, C. P. (1985). Sociopathy and psychotherapy outcome. *Archives of General Psychiatry, 42*, 1081–1086. http://dx.doi.org/10.1001/archpsyc.1985.01790340059009

World Health Organization (1993). *International classification of diseases* (10th ed.). Geneva, Switzerland: Author.

Wright, A. G. C., Pincus, A. L., & Lenzenweger, M. F. (2012). An empirical examination of distributional assumptions underlying the relationship between personality disorder symptoms and personality traits. *Journal of Abnormal Psychology, 121*, 699–706. http://dx.doi.org/10.1037/a0029042

Young, J. E., Klosko, J. S., & Weishaar, M. E. (2003). *Schema therapy: A practitioner's guide.* New York, NY: Guilford Press.

Zanarini, M. C. (2000). Childhood experiences associated with the development of borderline personality disorder. *Psychiatric Clinics of North America, 23*, 89–101. http://dx.doi.org/10.1016/S0193-953X(05)70145-3

Zanarini, M. C. (2008). Reasons for change in borderline personality disorder (and other Axis II disorders). *Psychiatric Clinics of North America, 31*, 505–515, viii. http://dx.doi.org/10.1016/j.psc.2008.03.006

Zanarini, M. C. (2009). Psychotherapy of borderline personality disorder. *Acta Psychiatrica Scandinavica, 120*, 373–377.

Zanarini, M. C., Frankenburg, F. R., Dubo, E. D., Sickel, A. E., Trikha, A., Levin, A., & Reynolds, V. (1998). Axis I comorbidity of borderline personality disorder. *The American Journal of Psychiatry, 155*, 1733–1739.

Zanarini, M. C., Frankenburg, F. R., Khera, G. S., & Bleichmar, J. (2001). Treatment histories of borderline inpatients. *Comprehensive Psychiatry, 42*, 144–150. http://dx.doi.org/10.1053/comp.2001.19749

Zanarini, M. C., Frankenburg, F., Reich, B., & Fitzmaurice, G. (2012). Attainment and stability of sustained symptomatic remission and recovery among patients with borderline personality and Axis II comparison subjects: A 16-year prospective follow-up study. *The American Journal of Psychiatry, 169*, 476–483. http://dx.doi.org/10.1176/appi.ajp.2011.11101550

Zanarini, M. C., Frankenburg, F. R., Reich, D. B., Silk, K. R., Hudson, J. I., & McSweeney, L. B. (2007). The subsyndromal phenomenology of borderline personality disorder: A 10-year follow-up study. *The American Journal of Psychiatry, 164*, 929–935.

Zanarini, M. C., Frankenburg, F. R., Wedig, M. M., & Fitzmaurice, G. M. (2013). Cognitive experiences reported by patients with borderline personality disorder and Axis II comparison subjects: A 16-year prospective follow-up study. *The American Journal of Psychiatry, 170*, 671–679. http://dx.doi.org/10.1176/appi.ajp.2013.13010055

Zanarini, M. C., Gunderson, J. G., & Frankenburg, F. R. (1990). Cognitive features of borderline personality disorder. *The American Journal of Psychiatry, 147*, 57–63.

Zanarini, M. C., Gunderson, J. G., Frankenburg, F. R., & Chauncey, D. L. (1989). The revised Diagnostic Interview for Borderlines: Discriminating BPD from other Axis II disorders. *Journal of Personality Disorders, 3*, 10–18.

Zanarini, M. C., Horwood, J., Wolke, D., Waylen, A., Fitzmaurice, G., & Grant, B. F. (2011). Prevalence of *DSM–IV* borderline personality disorder in two community samples: 6,330 English 11-year-olds and 34,653 American adults. *Journal of Personality Disorders, 25,* 607–619. http://dx.doi.org/10.1521/pedi.2011.25.5.607

Zelkowitz, P., Paris, J., Guzder, J., Feldman, R., Roy, C., & Rosval, L. (2007). A five-year follow-up of patients with borderline pathology of childhood. *Journal of Personality Disorders: Theory, Research and Treatment, 21,* 664–674. http://dx.doi.org/10.1521/pedi.2007.21.6.664

Zimmerman, M. (2012). Is there adequate empirical justification for radically revising the personality disorders section for *DSM-5? Personality Disorders: Theory, Research, and Treatment, 3,* 444–457. http://dx.doi.org/10.1037/a0022108

Zimmerman, M., Chelminski, I., Young, D., Dalrymple, K., & Martinez, J. (2013). Is dimensional scoring of borderline personality disorder important only for subthreshold levels of severity? *Journal of Personality Disorders, 27,* 244–251. http://dx.doi.org/10.1521/pedi_2012_26_022

Zimmerman, M., Dalrymple, K., Chelminski, I., Young, D., & Galione, J. N. (2010). Recognition of irrationality of fear and the diagnosis of social anxiety disorder and specific phobia in adults: Implications for criteria revision in *DSM–5. Depression and Anxiety, 27,* 1044–1049. http://dx.doi.org/10.1002/da.20716

Zimmerman, M., & Mattia, J. I. (1999). Differences between clinical and research practices in diagnosing borderline personality disorder. *The American Journal of Psychiatry, 156,* 1570–1574.

Zimmerman, M., Rothschild, L., & Chelminski, I. (2005). The prevalence of *DSM–IV* personality disorders in psychiatric outpatients. *The American Journal of Psychiatry, 162,* 1911–1918. http://dx.doi.org/10.1176/appi.ajp.162.10.1911

Zoccolillo, M., Pickles, A., Quinton, D., & Rutter, M. (1992). The outcome of childhood conduct disorder: Implications for defining adult personality disorder and conduct disorder. *Psychological Medicine, 22,* 971–986. http://dx.doi.org/10.1017/S003329170003854X

Zweig-Frank, H., & Paris, J. (1991). Parents' emotional neglect and overprotection according to the recollections of patients with borderline personality disorder. *The American Journal of Psychiatry, 148,* 648–651.

Index

Addictions, 76

ADHD. *See* Attention-deficit/
    hyperactivity disorder

Adolescent onset, 86–88, 155–156

Affective instability, 74–75, 77–79, 84

Alexander, F., 139

American Journal of Psychiatry, 31, 32

American Psychiatric Association, 116

Anorexia nervosa, 25

Antidepressants, 111–114

Antiepileptic agents, 114

Antipsychotics, 115–116

Antisocial personality disorder (APD),
    65–71
  case example, 65–66
  characteristics and traits of, 29–30,
      67–68
  childhood precursors of, 58
  context of, 24
  history of, 66–67
  management of, 70–71
  outcomes with, 61, 70
  prevalence of, 51, 55–56, 68, 156
  research on, 51
  risk factors for, 68–70
  size of research on, 6

APD. *See* Antisocial personality
    disorder

Attachment theory, 124

Attention-deficit/hyperactivity
    disorder (ADHD)
  and borderline personality
      disorder, 82
  medications for treating, 13
  misdiagnosis of, 13, 16

Atypical antipsychotics, 115–116

Auditory hallucinations, 80

Avoidant personality disorder
  length of treatment for patients
      with, 138
  outcomes with, 61
  overview, 102–103
  research on, 100

Awareness campaigns, 158–159

Axis II disorders, 35. *See also* Personal-
    ity disorders

Balsis, S., 28

Barratt, E. S., 78

Bateman, Anthony, 125, 132, 145

Batstra, L., 82

Baumgard, C. H., 70

Behavioral genetics. *See* Genetics,
    behavioral

Behavioral inhibition, 60

Bell, S. E., 70

Belsky, J., 48, 59

Bias, gender, 102

Big Five. *See* Five-factor model of personality
Biological factors, 45–47, 157
Biological reductionism, 14–15
Biomarkers, 44–45
Biomedical approaches, 17
Biopsychosocial models, 83–86, 153–154
Biparental failure, 50
Bipolar disorder, 16, 81–82, 114
Bipolarity, 78
Black, D. W., 70
Bleichmar, J., 86
Borderline personality disorder (BPD), 73–89
    biopsychosocial model of, 83–86
    body of research on, 6, 154, 158
    case example, 73
    and childhood adversity, 48–51
    childhood precursors of, 58–60, 86–88, 155
    clinical features of, 74–82
    cognitive symptoms in, 75, 80–81
    dialectical behavior therapy for treatment of. *See* Dialectical behavior therapy
    differential diagnosis of, 81–82
    genetic basis for, 45
    impulsivity in, 78–79
    management of suicidality with, 78–79, 88, 146–149
    mood features of, 77–78
    neuroimaging research on, 47, 83
    outcomes with, 61, 88–89
    pharmacotherapy for treatment of, 114–117
    prevalence of, 52, 56, 82
    stepped care model for treatment of, 142–145
    substance abuse comorbid with, 141
    traits of, 28–29
    treatment options for, 88
Bornstein, Robert, 103

BPD. *See* Borderline personality disorder
Brain research, 68–69. *See also* Neuroimaging research

"Capacity to mentalize," 132
Caspi, A., 69
Categorical models, 20
CBT (cognitive behavior therapy), 96–97, 121, 126
Chain analysis, 121
Chelminski, I., 57, 70
Childhood adversity, 48–51, 84
Childhood precursors, 58–60, 86–88, 155
Childhood sexual abuse (CSA), 48–49
Children in the Community Study, 59
Chronicity of personality disorders, 60, 139
Cicchetti, D., 49, 85
Cleckley, Hervey, 66–67
CLPS. *See* Collaborative Longitudinal Personality Disorders Study
Cochrane group, 112, 114, 117, 130
Cognitive analytic therapy, 126
Cognitive behavior therapy (CBT), 96–97, 121, 126
Cohen, J., 60
Cohen, P., 60
Collaborative Longitudinal Personality Disorders Study (CLPS), 27, 31, 61–62, 100, 101
Common final pathway, 85
Complex trauma, 84
Conduct disorder (CD), 58, 67
Contracts, therapy, 139, 140
Cooper, L. D., 28
Criminality, 68–71. *See also* Antisocial personality disorder
CSA (childhood sexual abuse), 48–49
Cyclothymic personality, 100

DBT. *See* Dialectical behavior therapy
Dependent personality disorder, 99, 103

Depression, 15–16, 18, 76, 81, 113. *See also* Antidepressants
Diagnosis. *See* Personality disorder diagnosis
Diagnostic and Statistical Manual of Mental Disorders (DSM–I), 66
Diagnostic and Statistical Manual of Mental Disorders (DSM–III), 35, 55, 92, 102
Diagnostic and Statistical Manual of Mental Disorders (DSM–5)
  antisocial personality disorder criteria in, 67
  borderline personality disorder criteria in, 80
  and dimensional approach to PDs, 30–36
  major depression in, 15–16
  narcissistic personality disorder in, 92
  personality disorders in, 4, 18–19, 58, 154–155
  schizotypal and related PDs in, 99–101
Diagnostic Assessment of Personality Pathology, 28
Diagnostic Interview for Borderlines, Revised (DIB–R), 80–81
Dialectical behavior therapy (DBT), 89, 121–124, 141, 143, 157–158
Differential susceptibility, 154
Dimensional assessment, 25–36
  DSM–5 controversy over, 30–36
  reluctance toward adoption of, 19–20
  research on, 20
Dissocial personality, 66
Dobbs, S., 48
Domestic violence, 71
Dougherty, D. M., 78
DSM. See Diagnostic and Statistical Manual of Mental Disorders headings

Dysphoria, 75

Eating disorders, 25, 76
ECA (Epidemiological Catchment Area) study, 55–56
Egodystonic aspects of PDs, 25–30
Ego strengths, 120
Egosyntonic aspects of PDs, 25–30
Eli Lilly, 116
Emotion dysregulation, 77, 114–115, 121, 134–135
Emotional dysregulation disorder, 74
Empathy, 71, 93, 131
Epidemiological Catchment Area (ECA) study, 55–56
Equifinality, 49, 85
Etiology of personality disorders, 41–53
  biological factors, 45–47
  biopsychosocial models of, 83–86, 153–154
  childhood adversity in, 48–51
  integrated models of, 52–53
  and personality traits, 42–45
  psychological factors, 47–48
  social factors, 51–52
  temperament's role in, 41–42
Evidence-based treatments, 124–129, 133–135
Externalizing disorders, 59

Family dysfunction, 69, 84
Five-factor model of personality
  applications of, 38
  Conscientiousness in, 104
  overview, 19, 24
  self-report questionnaires based on, 43–45
Fonagy, P., 125, 132
Frances, A., 82
Frankenburg, F. R., 86
French, T., 139
Freud, S., 139
Fundamental attribution bias, 12

Gender bias, 102
Gender differences, 82
General psychiatric management, 123
Genetics, behavioral, 44
    of antisocial personality disorder, 69
    of borderline personality
        disorder, 45
    future directions for research, 157
    of narcissistic personality
        disorder, 96
Goodman, M., 83
"Good psychiatric management," 127
Grant, B. F., 57
Group therapy, 121, 125, 133
Gunderson, J. G., 79, 80, 127

Hallucinations, 80
Hare, Robert, 67
Harmful dysfunction, 20
Heritability, 41–43, 45–47, 83. *See also*
    Genetics, behavioral
Histrionic personality disorder, 99,
    101–102
Hospitalization, 146–147
Hypomania, 77
Hysteria, 101–102

*ICD–11. See International Classification
    of Diseases*
Impulsivity, 69, 78–79, 130
Individualism, 95
Insel, Thomas R., 14–15, 37
Insomnia, 130
Interminable therapy, 138–140
Internalizing disorders, 59
International Classification of Diseases
    (*ICD–11*), 36–37, 66, 92, 99
International Society for the Study of
    Personality Disorders, 5

Journal of Personality Disorders, 5

Kagan, J., 24, 42, 60
Khera, G. S., 86

Koenigsberg, H. W., 132
Kohut, Heinz, 97
Kupfer, D. J., 36

Lasch, Christopher, 95
Lenzenweger, M. F., 27
Linehan, M.
    conceptualization of BPD by, 50,
        85
    and history of dialectical behavior
        therapy, 119, 121, 124, 131,
        132, 134
    importance of work done by, 154
    skills-based approach developed
        by, 140
Links, P. R., 127
Lithium, 114
Livesley, W. John, 32, 33, 124, 128
Loneliness, 138
Longitudinal Personality Disorders
    Study. *See* Collaborative
    Longitudinal Personality
    Disorders Study
Lyons-Ruth, K., 79

Major depression. *See* Depression
Management, 137–152
    case examples, 149–152
    and length of therapy, 138–140
    philosophy of, 152
    principles for, 140–141
    stepped care model for, 142–145
    of suicidality accompanying BPD,
        146–149
The Mask of Sanity (Hervey
    Cleckley), 66
Mattia, J. I., 60
MBT (mentalization-based treat-
    ment), 124–125, 134–135, 145
McGrath, R. E., 111
McLean Hospital, 80
McLean Study of Adult Development,
    61–62
McMain, S. F., 122–123

INDEX

Medication. *See* Psychopharmacology
Mentalization-based treatment
(MBT), 124–125, 134–135, 145
Millon, Theodore, 102
Misdiagnosis, 15–17
Moeller, F. G., 78
Monoamine oxidase inhibitors, 114
Mood disorders, 17–18. *See also*
specific mood disorders
Mood stabilizers, 114–115
"Moral insanity," 66
Moran, P., 68
Morey, L. C., 27
Multifinality, 85

Narcissistic personality disorder
(NPD), 91–97
case example, 91
clinical features of, 93
history of, 92–93
prevalence of, 52, 94–95
risk factors for, 96
risks and benefits of, 93–94
traits of, 26, 29
treatment for, 96–97
Narcissistic Personality Interview
(NPI), 95
National Epidemiological Survey on
Alcohol and Related Conditions
(NESARC), 56, 68, 94, 104
National Health Service (United
Kingdom), 71
National Institute for Clinical
Excellence, 114, 116
National Institute of Mental Health
(NIMH), 37, 61
NESARC. *See* National Epidemio-
logical Survey on Alcohol and
Related Conditions
Neuroimaging research
on borderline personality disorder,
47, 83
on re-experiencing trauma, 132
Neuroleptics, 115–116

Neuroscience models of pathology,
14–15
New, A. S., 83
NIMH (National Institute of Mental
Health), 37
NPD. *See* Narcissistic personality
disorder
NPI (Narcissistic Personality
Interview), 95

Obsessive–compulsive disorder, 25
Obsessive–compulsive personality
disorder (OCPD)
outcomes with, 61, 100
overview, 103–104
prevalence of, 57
traits of, 26, 29
Oltmanns, T. F., 28
Open-ended therapy, 138–140
Outcomes, 60–62
with antisocial personality disorder,
61, 70
with borderline personality
dis-order, 61, 88–89
with obsessive–compulsive personality disorder, 61, 100
Overdoses, 75

Paranoia, 80
Paranoid personality disorder,
99–101
Parental Bonding Index (PBI), 50
Parker, G., 50
PCL–R (Psychopathy Checklist), 67
PD-NOS (personality disorder not
otherwise specified), 19, 104
PDs. *See* Personality disorders
Personality disorder diagnosis, 11–21,
23–39
and complexity of personality,
17–18
dimensional approach to. *See*
Dimensional assessment
DSM–5 controversy over, 30–36

egosyntonic and egodystonic
aspects in, 25–30
future of, 36–38
misdiagnosis, 15–17
need for changes in, 38–39
and neuroscience models of
pathology, 14–15
normal personality variation vs.,
18–21
personality traits vs., 23–25
stigma carried with, 11–14
underdiagnosis, 3–4
Personality disorder not otherwise
specified (PD-NOS), 19, 104
Personality disorders (PDs). *See also
specific headings*
management of, 3
myths and realities about, 159–160
*Personality Disorders: Theory, Research,
and Treatment,* 38
Personality variations, 18–21
Pincus, A. L., 27
Pittsburgh Girls Study, 59
Pluess, M., 48
Polypharmacy, 116–117
Posttraumatic stress disorder (PTSD),
16, 76
Prevalence
of antisocial personality disorder,
51, 55–56, 68, 156
of borderline personality disorder,
52, 56, 82
epidemiological studies on, 55–57
future directions for research on,
156
of narcissistic personality disorder,
52, 94–95
of obsessive–compulsive personality disorder, 57
Prevention, 155
Psychoanalysis, 92, 96
Psychopathy, 66
Psychopathy Checklist (PCL–R), 67
Psychopharmacology, 109–117

with antidepressants, 113–114
with antipsychotics, 115–116
ineffective treatment with, 13
with mood stabilizers, 114–115
overuse of, 130
polypharmacy, 116–117
rationale for, 110–113
Psychotherapy, 119–135
accessibility of, 157–158
agents of change in, 130–133
dialectical behavior therapy. *See*
Dialectical behavior therapy
evidence-based treatments for
BPD, 124–129, 133–135
importance of structure in, 120,
129–130
length of treatment in, 138–140
psychiatrists' declining use of, 111
for treatment of antisocial personality disorder, 71
for treatment of borderline
personality disorder, 89
for treatment of narcissistic
personality disorder, 96–97
PTSD (posttraumatic stress disorder),
16, 76

Quirion, R., 14–15

Radical acceptance, 121, 132
Raine, Adrian, 68
Regier, D. A., 36
Research Domain Criteria (RDoC), 37
Resilience, 43, 47
Robins, Lee, 67
Rogosch, F. A., 49, 85
Rothschild, L., 57, 70
Rutter, Michael, 41

Schedule for Nonadaptive and
Adaptive Personality, 28
Schema-focused therapy, 126
Schizoid personality disorder, 99–101
Schizophrenia, 61, 74, 99

Schizotypal personality disorder,
99–101
Schmitz, J. M., 78
Selective serotonin reuptake inhibitors
(SSRIs), 114
Self-harm, 75, 79
Self-report instruments, 28, 43–45
Siever, Larry J., 83, 99
"Simple schizophrenia," 100
Singer, M. T., 80
Skills learning, 140–141
Skodol, Andrew, 31
Social capital, 141
Sociopathic personality, 66
Sociopathy, 66
SSRIs (selective serotonin reuptake
inhibitors), 114
Stepped care models, 142–145
STEPPS (systems training for emo-
tional predictability and prob-
lem solving), 127, 133, 134
Stern, Adolf, 74
Stigma, personality disorder, 11–14
Stone, M. H., 89
Stress–diathesis model, 86
Substance abuse, 71, 141
Suicidality, 78–79, 88, 146–149
Susceptibility, differential, 154
Swann, A. C., 78
Systems training for emotional pre-
dictability and problem solving
(STEPPS), 127, 133, 134

TAU. *See* Treatment as usual
Temperament, 41–42, 58
TFP (transference-focused psycho-
therapy), 125

Therapy contracts, 139, 140
Torgersen, S., 102, 103
Traits
of antisocial personality disorder,
29–30
boundaries between disorders and,
23–25
and etiology of PDs, 42–45
of narcissistic personality disorder,
26, 29
Transference-focused psychotherapy
(TFP), 125
Trauma
and borderline personality
disorder, 84–85
complex, 84
reexperiencing of, 132
Treatment. *See specific forms of
treatment, e.g.,* Psycho-
pharmacology
Treatment as usual (TAU), 120–121,
125–127, 131
Treatment-resistance depression, 113
Tricyclic antidepressants, 114
Triebwasser, J., 83
Twenge, J. M., 95

Underdiagnosis, 3–4

Wakefield, J. C., 20
Widiger, Tom, 38–39
World Health Organization (WHO), 36
Wright, A. G. C., 27

Zanarini, M. C., 27, 86
Zimmerman, M., 36, 57, 60, 70,
101–104

About the Author

Joel Paris, MD, PhD, was born in New York City but has spent most of his life in Canada. He earned an MD from McGill University in 1964, where he also trained in psychiatry. Dr. Paris has been a member of the McGill psychiatry department since 1972, where he is a full professor and has served as department chair.

Dr. Paris's research interest is in borderline personality disorder. Over the past 20 years, he has conducted research on its causes and outcome. He has published more than 200 peer-reviewed articles and book chapters and is the author of 18 previous books. Dr. Paris is also an educator who has won awards for his teaching and is the former editor-in-chief of the *Canadian Journal of Psychiatry.*